DR. FAUSTUS

By CHRISTOPHER MARLOWE

Dr. Faustus
By Christopher Marlowe

Print ISBN 13: 978-1-4209-6103-4
eBook ISBN 13: 978-1-4209-6030-3

Cover Image: a detail of "Doctor Faust" (chromolitho), Spanish School, (19th century) / Private Collection / © Look and Learn / Bridgeman Images.

Please visit *www.digireads.com*

CONTENTS

INTRODUCTORY NOTE

Christopher Marlowe, the author of the earliest dramatic version of the Faust legend, was the son of a shoemaker in Canterbury, where he was born in February, 1564, some two months before Shakespeare. After graduating as M.A. from the University of Cambridge in 1587, he seems to have settled in London; and that same year is generally accepted as the latest date for the production of his tragedy of "Tamburlaine," the play which is regarded as having established blank verse as the standard meter of the English Drama. "Doctor Faustus" probably came next in 1588, followed by "The Jew of Malta" and "Edward II." Marlowe had a share in the production of several other plays, wrote the first two sestiads of "Hero and Leander," and made translations from Ovid and Lucan. He met his death in a tavern brawl, June 1, 1593.

Of Marlowe personally little is known. The common accounts of his atheistical beliefs and dissipated life are probably exaggerated, recent researches having given ground for believing that his heterodoxy may have amounted to little more than a form of Unitarianism. Some of the attacks on his character are based on the evidence of witnesses whose reputation will not bear investigation, while the character of some of his friends and their manner of speaking of him are of weight on the other side.

The most striking feature of Marlowe's dramas is the concentration of interest on an impressive central figure dominated by a single passion, the thirst for the unattainable. In "Tamburlaine" this takes the form of universal power; in "The Jew of Malta," infinite riches; in "Doctor Faustus" universal knowledge. The aspirations of these dominant personalities are uttered in sonorous blank verse, and in a rhetoric which at times rises to the sublime, at times descends to rant. "Doctor Faustus," though disfigured by poor comic scenes for which Marlowe is probably not responsible, and though lacking unity of structure, yet presents the career and fate of the hero with great power, and contains in the speech to Helen of Troy and in the dying utterance of Faustus two of the most superb passages of poetry in the English language.

DOCTOR FAUSTUS, 1604, THE "A" TEXT

DRAMATIS PERSONAE

THE POPE.
CARDINAL OF LORRAIN.
EMPEROR OF GERMANY.
DUKE OF VANHOLT.
FAUSTUS.
VALDES AND CORNELIUS, FRIENDS TO FAUSTUS.
WAGNER, SERVANT TO FAUSTUS.
CLOWN.
ROBIN.
RALPH.
VINTNER,
HORSE-COURSER,
KNIGHT,
OLD MAN,
SCHOLARS, FRIARS, AND ATTENDANTS.
DUCHESS OF VANHOLT.
LUCIFER.
BELZEBUB.
MEPHISOPHILIS.
GOOD ANGEL,
EVIL ANGEL,
THE SEVEN DEADLY SINS,
DEVILS, SPIRITS IN THE SHAPE OF ALEXANDER THE GREAT, OF HIS
     PARAMOUR, AND OF HELEN OF TROY.
CHORUS.

THE TRAGICAL HISTORY OF DOCTOR FAUSTUS

FROM THE QUARTO OF 1604.

[*Enter* CHORUS.]

CHORUS. Not marching now in fields of Trasimene,
　　Where Mars did mate[1] the Carthaginians;
　　Nor sporting in the dalliance of love,
　　In courts of kings where state is overturn'd;
　　Nor in the pomp of proud audacious deeds,
　　Intends our Muse to vaunt his heavenly verse:
　　Only this, gentlemen,—we must perform
　　The form of Faustus' fortunes, good or bad.
　　To patient judgments we appeal our plaud,[2]
　　And speak for Faustus in his infancy.
　　Now is he born, his parents base of stock,
　　In Germany, within a town call'd Rhodes;[3]
　　Of riper years to Wittenberg he went,
　　Whereas his kinsmen chiefly brought him up.
　　So soon he profits in divinity,
　　The fruitful plot of scholarism grac'd,[4]
　　That shortly he was grac'd with doctor's name,
　　Excelling all those sweet delight disputes
　　In heavenly matters of theology;
　　Till swollen with cunning,[5] of a self-conceit,
　　His waxen wings[6] did mount above his reach,
　　And, melting, Heavens conspir'd his overthrow;
　　For, falling to a devilish exercise,
　　And glutted [now] with learning's golden gifts,
　　He surfeits upon cursed necromancy.
　　Nothing so sweet as magic is to him,
　　Which he prefers before his chiefest bliss.
　　And this the man that in his study sits! [*Exit.*]

---

[1] Confound. But Hannibal was victorious at Lake Trasimenus, B. C. 217.
[2] For applause.
[3] Roda, in the Duchy of Saxe-Altenburg, near Jena.
[4] The garden of scholarship being adorned by him.
[5] Knowledge.
[6] An allusion to the myth of Icarus, who flew too near the sun.

SCENE I.

[FAUSTUS *discovered in his Study.*]

FAUSTUS. Settle my studies, Faustus, and begin
To sound the depth of that thou wilt profess;[7]
Having commenc'd, be a divine in show,
Yet level[8] and at the end of every art,
And live and die in Aristotle's works.
Sweet Analytics,[9] 'tis thou hast ravish'd me,
Bene disserere est finis logices.[10]
Is to dispute well logic's chiefest end?
Affords this art no greater miracle?
Then read no more, thou hast attain'd the end;
A greater subject fitteth Faustus' wit.
Bid ὄν καίμή ὄν[11] farewell; Galen come,
Seeing *Ubi desinit Philosophus ibi incipit Medicus;*[12]
Be a physician, Faustus, heap up gold,
And be eternis'd for some wondrous cure.
Summum bonum medicinæ sanitas,[13]
"The end of physic is our body's health"
Why, Faustus, hast thou not attain'd that end!
Is not thy common talk sound Aphorisms?[14]
Are not thy bills[15] hung up as monuments,
Whereby whole cities have escap'd the plague,
And thousand desperate maladies been eas'd?
Yet art thou still but Faustus and a man.
Couldst thou make men to live eternally,
Or, being dead, raise them to life again,
Then this profession were to be esteem'd.
Physic, farewell.—Where is Justinian? [*Reads.*]
Si una eademque res legatur duobus, alter rem, alter valorem rei,
    &c.[16]

---

[7] Teach publicly.
[8] Aim.
[9] Logic.
[10] "To argue well is the end of logic."
[11] This is Mr. Bullen's emendation of Q1., Oncaymæon, a corruption of the Aristotelian phrase for "being and not being."
[12] "Where the philosopher leaves off, there the physician begins."
[13] This and the previous quotation are from Aristotle.
[14] Medical maxims.
[15] Announcements.
[16] "If one and the same thing is bequeathed to two person, one gets the thing and the other the value of the thing."

A pretty case of paltry legacies! [*Reads.*]
Ex hæreditare filium non potest pater nisi, &c.[17]
Such is the subject of the Institute[18]
And universal Body of the Law.[19]
His[20] study fits a mercenary drudge,
Who aims at nothing but external trash;
Too servile and illiberal for me.
When all is done, divinity is best;
Jerome's Bible,[21] Faustus, view it well. [*Reads.*]
Stipendium peccati mors est. Ha! *Stipendium, &c.*
"The reward of sin is death." That's hard. [*Reads.*]
Si peccasse negamus fallimur et nulla est in nobis veritas.
"If we say that we have no sin we deceive ourselves, and there's no
    truth in us." Why then, belike we must sin and so
    consequently die.
Ay, we must die an everlasting death.
What doctrine call you this, *Che sera sera,*
"What will be shall be?" Divinity, adieu
These metaphysics of magicians
And necromantic books are heavenly;
Lines, circles, scenes, letters, and characters,
Ay, these are those that Faustus most desires.
O what a world of profit and delight,
Of power, of honour, of omnipotence
Is promised to the studious artisan!
All things that move between the quiet poles
Shall be at my command. Emperor and kings
Are but obeyed in their several provinces,
Nor can they raise the wind or rend the clouds;
But his dominion that exceeds[22] in this
Stretcheth as far as doth the mind of man.
A sound magician is a mighty god:
Here, Faustus, try thy[23] brains to gain a deity.
Wagner!

[*Enter* WAGNER.]

---

[17] "A father cannot disinherit the son except," etc.
[18] Of Justinian, under whom the Roman law was codified.
[19] Q1., Church.
[20] Its.
[21] The Vulgate.
[22] Excels.
[23] Q3., tire my.

Commend me to my dearest friends,
The German Valdes and Cornelius;
Request them earnestly to visit me.

WAGNER. I will, sir. Exit.
FAUSTUS. Their conference will be a greater help to me
Than all my labours, plod I ne'er so fast.

[*Enter* GOOD ANGEL *and* EVIL ANGEL.]

GOOD ANGEL. O Faustus! lay that damned book aside,
And gaze not upon it lest it tempt thy soul,
And heap God's heavy wrath upon thy head.
Read, read the Scriptures: that is blasphemy.
EVIL ANGEL. Go forward, Faustus, in that famous art,
Wherein all Nature's treasure is contain'd:
Be thou on earth as Jove is in the sky,
Lord and commander of these elements.

[*Exeunt* ANGELS.]

FAUSTUS. How am I glutted with conceit[24] of this!
Shall I make spirits fetch me what I please,
Resolve me of all ambiguities,
Perform what desperate enterprise I will?
I'll have them fly to India for gold,
Ransack the ocean for orient pearl,
And search all corners of the new-found world
For pleasant fruits and princely delicates;
I'll have them read me strange philosophy
And tell the secrets of all foreign kings;
I'll have them wall all Germany with brass,
And make swift Rhine circle fair Wittenberg;
I'll have them fill the public schools with silk,[25]
Wherewith the students shall be bravely clad;
I'll levy soldiers with the coin they bring,
And chase the Prince of Parma from our land,[26]
And reign sole king of all the provinces;
Yea, stranger engines for the brunt of war
Than was the fiery keel[27] at Antwerp's bridge,

---

[24] Idea.
[25] Qq., skill.
[26] The Netherlands, over which Parma re-established the Spanish dominions.

I'll make my servile spirits to invent.

[*Enter* VALDES *and* CORNELIUS.[28]]

Come, German Valdes and Cornelius,
And make me blest with your sage conference.
Valdes, sweet Valdes, and Cornelius,
Know that your words have won me at the last
To practise magic and concealed arts:
Yet not your words only, but mine own fantasy
That will receive no object, for my head
But ruminates on necromantic skill.
Philosophy is odious and obscure,
Both law and physic are for petty wits;
Divinity is basest of the three,
Unpleasant, harsh, contemptible, and vile:
'Tis magic, magic, that hath ravish'd me.
Then, gentle friends, aid me in this attempt;
And I that have with concise syllogisms
Gravell'd the pastors of the German church,
And made the flowering pride of Wittenberg
Swarm to my problems, as the infernal spirits
On sweet Musæus,[29] when he came to hell,
Will be as cunning as Agrippa was,
Whose shadows made all Europe honour him.
VALDES. Faustus, these books, thy wit, and our experience
Shall make all nations to canònise us.
As Indian Moors[30] obey their Spanish lords,
So shall the subjects[31] of every element
Be always serviceable to us three;
Like lions shall they guard us when we please;
Like Almain rutters[32] with their horsemen's staves
Or Lapland giants, trotting by our sides;
Sometimes like women or unwedded maids,
Shadowing more beauty in their airy brows
Than have the white breasts of the queen of love:
From Venice shall they drag huge argosies,
And from America the golden fleece

---

[27] A ship filled with explosives used to blow up a bridge built by Parma in 1585 at the siege of Antwerp.
[28] The famous Cornelius Agrippa. German Valdes is not known.
[29] Cf. Virgil, *Æn.* vi. 667; Dryden's trans. vi. 905 ff.
[30] American Indians.
[31] Q3., spirits.
[32] Troopers, Germ. *Reiters.*

That yearly stuffs old Philip's treasury;
   If learned Faustus will be resolute.
FAUSTUS. Valdes, as resolute am I in this
   As thou to live; therefore object is not.
CORNELIUS. The miracles that magic will perform
   Will make thee vow to study nothing else.
   He that is grounded in astrology,
   Enrich'd with tongues, as well seen[33] in minerals,
   Hath all the principles magic doth require.
   Then doubt not, Faustus, but to be renown'd,
   And more frequented for this mystery
   Than heretofore the Delphian Oracle.
   The spirits tell me they can dry the sea,
   And fetch the treasure of all foreign wrecks,
   Ay, all the wealth that our forefathers hid
   Within the massy entrails of the earth;
   Then tell me, Faustus, what shall we three want?
FAUSTUS. Nothing, Cornelius! O this cheers my soul!
   Come show me some demonstrations magical,
   That I may conjure in some lusty grove,
   And have these joys in full possession.
VALDES. Then haste thee to some solitary grove,
   And bear wise Bacon's[34] and Albanus'[35] works,
   The Hebrew Psalter and New Testament;
   And whatsoever else is requisite
   We will inform thee ere our conference cease.
CORNELIUS. Valdes, first let him know the words of art;
   And then, all other ceremonies learn'd,
   Faustus may try his cunning by himself.
VALDES. First I'll instruct thee in the rudiments,
   And then wilt thou be perfecter than I.
FAUSTUS. Then come and dine with me, and after meat,
   We'll canvass every quiddity thereof;
   For ere I sleep I'll try what I can do:
   This night I'll conjure though I die therefore. [*Exeunt.*]

---

[33] Versed.

[34] Roger Bacon.

[35] Perhaps Pietro d'Abano, a medieval alchemist; perhaps a misprint for Albertus (Magnus), the great schoolman.

SCENE II.

Before FAUSTUS'S *House.*

[*Enter two* SCHOLARS.]

FIRST SCHOLAR. I wonder what's become of Faustus that was wont to make our schools ring with *sic probo*?[36]
SECOND SCHOLAR. That shall we know, for see here comes his boy.

[*Enter* WAGNER.]

FIRST SCHOLAR. How now, sirrah! Where's thy master?
WAGNER. God in heaven knows!
SECOND SCHOLAR. Why, dost not thou know?
WAGNER. Yes, I know. But that follows not.
FIRST SCHOLAR. Go to, sirrah! Leave your jesting, and tell us where he is.
WAGNER. That follows not necessary by force of argument, that you, being licentiate, should stand upon't: therefore, acknowledge your error and be attentive.
SECOND SCHOLAR. Why, didst thou not say thou knew'st?
WAGNER. Have you any witness on't?
FIRST SCHOLAR. Yes, sirrah, I heard you.
WAGNER. Ask my fellow if I be a thief.
SECOND SCHOLAR. Well, you will not tell us?
WAGNER. Yes, sir, I will tell you; yet if you were not dunces, you would never ask me such a question; for is not he *corpus naturale*?[37] and is not that *mobile*? Then wherefore should you ask me such a question? But that I am by nature phlegmatic, slow to wrath, and prone to lechery (to love, I would say), it were not for you to come within forty feet of the place of execution, although I do not doubt to see you both hang'd the next sessions. Thus having triumph'd over you, I will set my countenance like a precisian,[38] and begin to speak thus:—Truly, my dear brethren, my master is within at dinner, with Valdes and Cornelius, as this wine, if it could speak, would inform your worships; and so the Lord bless you, preserve you, and keep you, my dear brethren, my dear brethren.
FIRST SCHOLAR. Nay, then, I fear he has fallen into that damned Art,

---

[36] "Thus I prove"—a common formula in scholastic discussions.
[37] "'*Corpus naturale seu mobile*' is the current scholastic expression for the subject-matter of physics."—Ward.
[38] Puritan.

for which they two are infamous through the world.

SECOND SCHOLAR. Were he a stranger, and not allied to me, yet should
I grieve for him. But come, let us go and inform the Rector, and
see if he by his grave counsel can reclaim him.

FIRST SCHOLAR. O, but I fear me nothing can reclaim him.

SECOND SCHOLAR. Yet let us try what we can do. [*Exeunt.*]

SCENE III.

A Grove.

[*Enter* FAUSTUS *to conjure.*]

FAUSTUS. Now that the gloomy shadow of the earth
  Longing to view Orion's drizzling look,
  Leaps from the antarctic world unto the sky,
  And dims the welkin with her pitchy breath,
  Faustus, begin thine incantations,
  And try if devils will obey thy hest,
  Seeing thou hast pray'd and sacrific'd to them.
  Within this circle is Jehovah's name,
  Forward and backward anagrammatis'd,
  The breviated names of holy saints,
  Figures of every adjunct to the Heavens,
  And characters of signs and erring[39] stars,
  By which the spirits are enforc'd to rise:
  Then fear not, Faustus, but be resolute,
  And try the uttermost magic can perform.

*Sint mihi Dei Acherontis propitii! Valeat numen triplex Jehovae!
Ignei, aerii, aquatani spiritus, salvete! Orientis princeps Belzebub,
inferni ardentis monarcha, et Demogorgon, propitiamus vos, ut
appareat et surgat Mephistophilis. Quid tu moraris? per Jehovam,
Gehennam et consecratum aquam quam nunc spargo, signumque
crucis quod nunc facio, et per vota nostra, ipse nunc surgat nobis
dicatus Mephistophilis!*[40]

[*Enter* MEPHISTOPHILIS, *a* DEVIL.]

---

[39] Wandering.

[40] "Be propitious to me, gods of Acheron! May the triple deity of Jehovah prevail!
Spirits of fire, air, water, hail! Belzebub, Prince of the East, monarch of burning hell, and
Demogorgon, we propitiate ye, that Mephistophilis may appear and rise. Why dost thou
delay? By Jehovah, Gehenna, and the holy water which now I sprinkle, and the sign of
the cross which now I make, and by our prayer, may Mephistophilis now summoned by
us arise!"

I charge thee to return and change thy shape;
Thou art too ugly to attend on me.
Go, and return an old Franciscan friar;
That holy shape becomes a devil best.

[*Exit* DEVIL.]

I see there's virtue in my heavenly words;
Who would not be proficient in this art?
How pliant is this Mephistophilis,
Full of obedience and humility!
Such is the force of magic and my spells.
[Now,] Faustus, thou art conjuror laureat,
Thou canst command great Mephistophilis:
Quin regis Mephistophilis fratris imagine.[41]

[*Re-enter* MEPHISTOPHILIS (*like a Franciscan Friar*).]

MEPHISTOPHILIS. Now, Faustus, what would'st thou have me to do?
FAUSTUS. I charge thee wait upon me whilst I live,
    To do whatever Faustus shall command,
    Be it to make the moon drop from her sphere,
    Or the ocean to overwhelm the world.
MEPHISTOPHILIS. I am a servant to great Lucifer,
    And may not follow thee without his leave
    No more than he commands must we perform.
FAUSTUS. Did not he charge thee to appear to me?
MEPHISTOPHILIS. No, I came hither of mine own accord.
FAUSTUS. Did not my conjuring speeches raise thee? Speak.
MEPHISTOPHILIS. That was the cause, but yet *per accidens*;
    For when we hear one rack[42] the name of God,
    Abjure the Scriptures and his Saviour Christ,
    We fly in hope to get his glorious soul;
    Nor will we come, unless he use such means
    Whereby he is in danger to be damn'd:
    Therefore the shortest cut for conjuring
    Is stoutly to abjure the Trinity,
    And pray devoutly to the Prince of Hell.
FAUSTUS. So Faustus hath
    Already done; and holds this principle,
    There is no chief but only Belzebub,

---

[41] "For indeed thou hast power in the image of thy brother Mephistophilis."
[42] Twist in anagrams.

To whom Faustus doth dedicate himself.
This word "damnation" terrifies not him,
For he confounds hell in Elysium;[43]
His ghost be with the old philosophers!
But, leaving these vain trifles of men's souls,
Tell me what is that Lucifer thy lord?
MEPHISTOPHILIS. Arch-regent and commander of all spirits.
FAUSTUS. Was not that Lucifer an angel once?
MEPHISTOPHILIS. Yes, Faustus, and most dearly lov'd of God.
FAUSTUS. How comes it then that he is Prince of devils?
MEPHISTOPHILIS. O, by aspiring pride and insolence;
    For which God threw him from the face of Heaven.
FAUSTUS. And what are you that you live with Lucifer?
MEPHISTOPHILIS. Unhappy spirits that fell with Lucifer,
    Conspir'd against our God with Lucifer,
    And are for ever damn'd with Lucifer.
FAUSTUS. Where are you damn'd?
MEPHISTOPHILIS. In hell.
FAUSTUS. How comes it then that thou art out of hell?
MEPHISTOPHILIS. Why this is hell, nor am I out of it.
    Think'st thou that I who saw the face of God,
    And tasted the eternal joys of Heaven,
    Am not tormented with ten thousand hells,
    In being depriv'd of everlasting bliss?
    O Faustus! leave these frivolous demands,
    Which strike a terror to my fainting soul.
FAUSTUS. What, is great Mephistophilis so passionate
    For being depriv'd of the joys of Heaven?
    Learn thou of Faustus manly fortitude,
    And scorn those joys thou never shalt possess.
    Go bear these tidings to great Lucifer:
    Seeing Faustus hath incurr'd eternal death
    By desperate thoughts against Jove's deity,
    Say he surrenders up to him his soul,
    So he will spare him four and twenty years,
    Letting him live in all voluptuousness;
    Having thee ever to attend on me;
    To give me whatsoever I shall ask,
    To tell me whatsoever I demand,
    To slay mine enemies, and aid my friends,
    And always be obedient to my will.
    Go and return to mighty Lucifer,
    And meet me in my study at midnight,

---

[43] Heaven and hell are indifferent to him.

And then resolve[44] me of thy master's mind.
MEPHISTOPHILIS. I will, Faustus. [*Exit.*]
FAUSTUS. Had I as many souls as there be stars,
    I'd give them all for Mephistophilis.
    By him I'll be great Emperor of the world,
    And make a bridge through the moving air,
    To pass the ocean with a band of men:
    I'll join the hills that bind the Afric shore,
    And make that [country] continent to Spain,
    And both contributory to my crown.
    The Emperor shall not live but by my leave,
    Nor any potentate of Germany.
    Now that I have obtain'd what I desire,
    I'll live in speculation[45] of this art
    Till Mephistophilis return again. [*Exit.*]

SCENE IV.

A Street.

[*Enter* WAGNER *and* CLOWN.]

WAGNER. Sirrah, boy, come hither.
CLOWN. How, boy! Swowns,[46] boy! I hope you have seen many boys
    with such pickadevaunts[47] as I have. Boy, quotha!
WAGNER. Tell me, sirrah, hast thou any comings in?
CLOWN. Ay, and goings out too. You may see else.
WAGNER. Alas, poor slave! See how poverty jesteth in his nakedness!
    The villain is bare and out of service, and so hungry that I know he
    would give his soul to the devil for a shoulder of mutton, though it
    were blood-raw.
CLOWN. How? My soul to the Devil for a shoulder of mutton, though
    'twere blood-raw! Not so, good friend. By'r Lady, I had need have
    it well roasted and good sauce to it, if I pay so dear.
WAGNER. Well, wilt thou serve me, and I'll make thee go like *Qui mihi*
    discipulus?[48]
CLOWN. How, in verse?
WAGNER. No, sirrah; in beaten silk and stavesacre.[49]

---

[44] Inform.
[45] Study.
[46] Zounds, i. e., God's wounds.
[47] Beards cut to a sharp point (Fr. *pic-à-devant*).
[48] Dyce points out that these are the first words of W. Lily's "*Ad discipulos carmen de moribus.*"
[49] A kind of larkspur, used for destroying lice.

CLOWN. How, how, Knave's acre!⁵⁰ Ay, I thought that was all the land his father left him. Do you hear? I would be sorry to rob you of your living.

WAGNER. Sirrah, I say in stavesacre.

CLOWN. Oho! Oho! Stavesacre! Why, then, belike if I were your man I should be full of vermin.

WAGNER. So thou shalt, whether thou beest with me or no. But, sirrah, leave your jesting, and bind yourself presently unto me for seven years, or I'll turn all the lice about thee into familiars, and they shall tear thee in pieces.

CLOWN. Do your hear, sir? You may save that labour; they are too familiar with me already. Swowns! they are as bold with my flesh as if they had paid for [their] meat and drink.

WAGNER. Well, do you hear, sirrah? Hold, take these guilders. [*Gives money.*]

CLOWN. Gridirons! what be they?

WAGNER. Why, French crowns.

CLOWN. Mass, but for the name of French crowns, a man were as good have as many English counters. And what should I do with these?

WAGNER. Why, now, sirrah, thou art at an hour's warning, whensoever and wheresoever the Devil shall fetch thee.

CLOWN. No, no. Here, take your gridirons again.

WAGNER. Truly I'll none of them.

CLOWN. Truly but you shall.

WAGNER. Bear witness I gave them him.

CLOWN. Bear witness I gave them you again.

WAGNER. Well, I will cause two devils presently to fetch thee away— Baliol and Belcher.

CLOWN. Let your Baliol and your Belcher come here, and I'll knock them, they were never so knock'd since they were devils. Say I should kill one of them, what would folks say? "Do you see yonder tall fellow in the round slop⁵¹—he has kill'd the devil." So I should be called Kill-devil all the parish over.

[*Enter two* DEVILS: *the* CLOWN *runs up and down crying.*]

WAGNER. Baliol and Belcher! Spirits, away!

[*Exeunt* DEVILS.]

CLOWN. What, are they gone? A vengeance on them, they have vile long nails! There was a he-devil, and a she-devil! I'll tell you how

---

⁵⁰ A mean street in London.
⁵¹ Short wide breeches.

you shall know them: all he-devils has horns, and all she-devils has clifts and cloven feet.

WAGNER. Well, sirrah, follow me.

CLOWN. But, do you hear—if I should serve you, would you teach me to raise up Banios and Belcheos?

WAGNER. I will teach thee to turn thyself to anything; to a dog, or a cat, or a mouse, or a rat, or anything.

CLOWN. How! a Christian fellow to a dog or a cat, a mouse or a rat! No, no, sir. If you turn me into anything, let it be in the likeness of a little pretty frisky flea, that I may be here and there and everywhere. Oh, I'll tickle the pretty wenches' plackets; I'll be amongst them, i' faith.

WAGNER. Well, sirrah, come.

CLOWN. But, do you hear, Wagner?

WAGNER. How! Baliol and Belcher!

CLOWN. O Lord! I pray, sir, let Banio and Belcher go sleep.

WAGNER. Villain—call me Master Wagner, and let thy left eye be diametarily[52] fixed upon my right heel, with *quasi vestigias nostras insistere.*[53] [*Exit.*]

CLOWN. God forgive me, he speaks Dutch fustian. Well, I'll follow him, I'll serve him, that's flat. [*Exit.*]

SCENE V.

[FAUSTUS *discovered in his Study.*]

FAUSTUS. Now, Faustus, must
Thou needs be damn'd, and canst thou not be sav'd:
What boots it then to think of God or Heaven?
Away with such vain fancies, and despair:
Despair in God, and trust in Belzebub.
Now go not backward: no, Faustus, be resolute.
Why waverest thou? O, something soundeth in mine ears
"Abjure this magic, turn to God again!"
Ay, and Faustus will turn to God again.
To God?—He loves thee not—
The God thou serv'st is thine own appetite,
Wherein is fix'd the love of Belzebub;
To him I'll build an altar and a church,
And offer lukewarm blood of new-born babes.

[*Enter* GOOD ANGEL *and* EVIL ANGEL.]

---

[52] For diametrically.
[53] "As if to tread in my tracks."

GOOD ANGEL. Sweet Faustus, leave that execrable art.
FAUSTUS. Contrition, prayer, repentance! What of them?
GOOD ANGEL. O, they are means to bring thee unto Heaven.
EVIL ANGEL. Rather, illusions, fruits of lunacy,
    That makes men foolish that do trust them most.
GOOD ANGEL. Sweet Faustus, think of Heaven, and heavenly things.
EVIL ANGEL. No, Faustus, think of honour and of wealth.

    [*Exeunt* ANGELS.]

FAUSTUS. Of wealth!
    What the signiory of Embden[54] shall be mine.
    When Mephistophilis shall stand by me,
    What God can hurt thee, Faustus? Thou art safe;
    Cast no more doubts. Come, Mephistophilis,
    And bring glad tidings from great Lucifer;—
    Is't not midnight? Come, Mephistophilis;
    Veni, veni, Mephistophile!

    [*Enter* MEPHISTOPHILIS.]

    Now tell me, what says Lucifer thy lord?
MEPHISTOPHILIS. That I shall wait on Faustus whilst he lives,
    So he will buy my service with his soul.
FAUSTUS. Already Faustus hath hazarded that for thee.
MEPHISTOPHILIS. But, Faustus, thou must bequeath it solemnly,
    And write a deed of gift with thine own blood,
    For that security craves great Lucifer.
    If thou deny it, I will back to hell.
FAUSTUS. Stay, Mephistophilis! and tell me what good
    Will my soul do thy lord.
MEPHISTOPHILIS. Enlarge his kingdom.
FAUSTUS. Is that the reason why he tempts us thus?
MEPHISTOPHILIS. *Solamen miseris socios habuisse doloris.*[55]
FAUSTUS. Why, have you any pain that torture others?
MEPHISTOPHILIS. As great as have the human souls of men.
    But tell me, Faustus, shall I have thy soul?
    And I will be thy slave, and wait on thee,
    And give thee more than thou hast wit to ask.
FAUSTUS. Ay, Mephistophilis, I give it thee.

---

    [54] Emden, near the mouth of the river Ems, was an important commercial town in Elizabethan times.
    [55] "Misery loves company."

MEPHISTOPHILIS. Then, Faustus, stab thine arm courageously.
  And bind thy soul that at some certain day
  Great Lucifer may claim it as his own;
  And then be thou as great as Lucifer.
FAUSTUS. [*Stabbing his arm.*] Lo, Mephistophilis, for love of thee,
  I cut mine arm, and with my proper blood
  Assure my soul to be great Lucifer's,
  Chief lord and regent of perpetual night!
  View here the blood that trickles from mine arm.
  And let it be propitious for my wish.
MEPHISTOPHILIS. But, Faustus, thou must
  Write it in manner of a deed of gift.
FAUSTUS. Ay, so I will. [*Writes.*] But, Mephistophilis,
  My blood congeals, and I can write no more.
MEPHISTOPHILIS. I'll fetch thee fire to dissolve it straight. [*Exit.*]
FAUSTUS. What might the staying of my blood portend?
  Is it unwilling I should write this bill?
  Why streams it not that I may write afresh?
  Faustus gives to thee his soul. Ah, there it stay'd.
  Why should'st thou not? Is not thy soul thine own?
  Then write again. *Faustus gives to thee his soul.*

  [*Re-enter* MEPHISTOPHILIS *with a chafer of coals.*]

MEPHISTOPHILIS. Here's fire. Come, Faustus, set it on.
FAUSTUS. So now the blood begins to clear again;
  [*Writes.*] Now will I make an end immediately.
MEPHISTOPHILIS. [*Aside.*]O what will not I do to obtain his soul.
FAUSTUS. *Consummatum est:*[56] this bill is ended,
  And Faustus hath bequeath'd his soul to Lucifer—
  But what is this inscription on mine arm?
  Homo, fuge![57] Whither should I fly?
  If unto God, he'll throw me down to hell.
  My senses are deceiv'd; here's nothing writ:—
  I see it plain; here in this place is writ
  Homo, fuge! Yet shall not Faustus fly.
MEPHISTOPHILIS. I'll fetch him somewhat to delight his mind. [*Exit.*]

  [*Re-enter* MEPHISTOPHILIS, *with* DEVILS, *giving crowns and rich
    apparel to* FAUSTUS, *dance, and depart.*]

---

[56] "It is finished."
[57] "Man, fly!"

FAUSTUS. Speak Mephistophilis, what means this show?
MEPHISTOPHILIS. Nothing, Faustus, but to delight thy mind withal,
    And to show thee what magic can perform.
FAUSTUS. But may I raise up spirits when I please?
MEPHISTOPHILIS. Ay, Faustus, and do greater things than these.
FAUSTUS. Then there's enough for a thousand souls.
    Here, Mephistophilis, receive this scroll,
    A deed of gift of body and of soul:
    But yet conditionally that thou perform
    All articles prescrib'd between us both.
MEPHISTOPHILIS. Faustus, I swear by hell and Lucifer
    To effect all promises between us made.
FAUSTUS. Then hear me read them: *On these conditions following.*
    First, that Faustus may be a spirit in form and substance.
    Secondly, that Mephistophilis shall be his servant, and at his
    command. Thirdly, that Mephistophilis shall do for him and bring
    him whatsoever [*he desires*]. *Fourthly, that he shall be in his*
    chamber or house invisible. Lastly, that he shall appear to the said
    John Faustus, at all times, and in what form or shape soever he
    pleases. I, John Faustus, of Wittenberg, Doctor, by these presents
    do give both body and soul to Lucifer, Prince of the East, and his
    minister, Mephistophilis; and furthermore grant unto them, that
    twenty-four years being expired, the articles above written
    inviolate, full power to fetch or carry the said John Faustus, body
    and soul, flesh, blood, or goods, into their habitation wheresoever.
    By me, John Faustus.
MEPHISTOPHILIS. Speak, Faustus, do you deliver this as your deed?
FAUSTUS. Ay, take it, and the Devil give thee good on't.
MEPHISTOPHILIS. Now, Faustus, ask what thou wilt.
FAUSTUS. First will I question with thee about hell.
    Tell me where is the place that men call hell?
MEPHISTOPHILIS. Under the Heaven.
FAUSTUS. Ay, but whereabout?
MEPHISTOPHILIS. Within the bowels of these elements,
    Where we are tortur'd and remain for ever;
    Hell hath no limits, nor is circumscrib'd
    In one self place; for where we are is hell,
    And where hell is there must we ever be:
    And, to conclude, when all the world dissolves,
    And every creature shall be purified,
    All places shall be hell that is not Heaven.
FAUSTUS. Come, I think hell's a fable.
MEPHISTOPHILIS. Ay, think so still, till experience change thy mind.
FAUSTUS. Why, think'st thou then that Faustus shall be damn'd?

MEPHISTOPHILIS. Ay, of necessity, for here's the scroll
    Wherein thou hast given thy soul to Lucifer.
FAUSTUS. Ay, and body too; but what of that?
    Think'st thou that Faustus is so fond[58] to imagine
    That, after this life, there is any pain?
    Tush; these are trifles, and mere old wives' tales.
MEPHISTOPHILIS. But, Faustus, I am an instance to prove the contrary,
    For I am damned, and am now in hell.
FAUSTUS. How! now in hell!
    Nay, an this be hell, I'll willingly be damn'd here;
    What? walking, disputing, &c.?
    But, leaving off this, let me have a wife,
    The fairest maid in Germany;
    For I am wanton and lascivious,
    And cannot live without a wife.
MEPHISTOPHILIS. How—a wife?
    I prithee, Faustus, talk not of a wife.
FAUSTUS. Nay, sweet Mephistophilis, fetch me one, for I will have one.
MEPHISTOPHILIS. Well—thou wilt have one. Sit there till I come:
    I'll fetch thee a wife in the Devil's name. [*Exit.*]

    [*Re-enter* MEPHISTOPHILIS *with a* DEVIL *dressed like a woman,
       with fireworks.*]

MEPHISTOPHILIS. Tell me, Faustus, how dost thou like thy wife?
FAUSTUS. A plague on her for a hot whore!
MEPHISTOPHILIS. Tut, Faustus,
    Marriage is but a ceremonial toy;
    And if thou lovest me, think no more of it.
    I'll cull thee out the fairest courtesans,
    And bring them every morning to thy bed;
    She whom thine eye shall like, thy heart shall have,
    Be she as chaste as was Penelope,
    As wise as Saba,[59] or as beautiful
    As was bright Lucifer before his fall.
    Here, take this book peruse it thoroughly: [*Gives a book.*]
    The iterating[60] of these lines brings gold;
    The framing of this circle on the ground
    Brings whirlwinds, tempests, thunder and lightning;
    Pronounce this thrice devoutly to thyself,
    And men in armour shall appear to thee,

---

[58] Foolish.
[59] The Queen of Sheba.
[60] Repeating.

Ready to execute what thou desir'st.

FAUSTUS. Thanks, Mephistophilis; yet fain would I have a book wherein I might behold all spells and incantations, that I might raise up spirits when I please.

MEPHISTOPHILIS. Here they are, in this book. [*Turns to them.*]

FAUSTUS. Now would I have a book where I might see all characters and planets of the heavens, that I might know their motions and dispositions.

MEPHISTOPHILIS. Here they are too. [*Turns to them.*]

FAUSTUS. Nay, let me have one book more,—and then I have done,— wherein I might see all plants, herbs, and trees that grow upon the earth.

MEPHISTOPHILIS. Here they be.

FAUSTUS. O, thou art deceived.

MEPHISTOPHILIS. Tut, I warrant thee. [*Turns to them. Exeunt.*]

SCENE VI.

The Same.

[*Enter* FAUSTUS *and* MEPHISTOPHILIS.]

FAUSTUS. When I behold the heavens, then I repent,
    And curse thee, wicked Mephistophilis,
    Because thou hast depriv'd me of those joys.

MEPHISTOPHILIS. Why, Faustus,
    Thinkest thou Heaven is such a glorious thing?
    I tell thee 'tis not half so fair as thou,
    Or any man that breathes on earth.

FAUSTUS. How provest thou that?

MEPHISTOPHILIS. 'Twas made for man, therefore is man more excellent.

FAUSTUS. If it were made for man, 'twas made for me:
    I will renounce this magic and repent.

[*Enter* GOOD ANGEL *and* EVIL ANGEL.]

GOOD ANGEL. Faustus, repent; yet God will pity thee.

EVIL ANGEL. Thou art a spirit; God can not pity thee.

FAUSTUS. Who buzzeth in mine ears I am a spirit?
    Be I a devil, yet God may pity me;
    Ay, God will pity me if I repent.

EVIL ANGEL. Ay, but Faustus never shall repent.

[*Exeunt* ANGELS.]

FAUSTUS. My heart's so hard'ned I cannot repent.
    Scarce can I name salvation, faith, or heaven,
    But fearful echoes thunder in mine ears
    "Faustus, thou art damn'd!" Then swords and knives,
    Poison, gun, halters, and envenom'd steel
    Are laid before me to despatch myself,
    And long ere this I should have slain myself,
    Had not sweet pleasure conquer'd deep despair.
    Have I not made blind Homer sing to me
    Of Alexander's love and Œnon's death?
    And hath not he that built the walls of Thebes
    With ravishing sound of his melodious harp,
    Made music with my Mephistophilis?
    Why should I die then, or basely despair?
    I am resolv'd: Faustus shall ne'er repent.
    Come, Mephistophilis, let us dispute again,
    And argue of divine astrology.
    Tell me, are there many heavens above the moon?
    Are all celestial bodies but one globe,
    As is the substance of this centric earth?
MEPHISTOPHILIS. As are the elements, such are the spheres
    Mutually folded in each other's orb,
    And, Faustus,
    All jointly move upon one axletree
    Whose terminine is termed the world's wide pole;
    Nor are the names of Saturn, Mars, or Jupiter
    Feign'd but are erring stars.
FAUSTUS. But tell me, have they all one motion, both *situ et tempore*?[61]
MEPHISTOPHILIS. All jointly move from east to west in twenty-four
    hours upon the poles of the world; but differ in their motion upon
    the poles of the zodiac.
FAUSTUS. Tush!
    These slender trifles Wagner can decide;
    Hath Mephistophilis no greater skill?
    Who knows not the double motion of the planets?
    The first is finish'd in a natural day;
        The second thus: as Saturn in thirty years; Jupiter in twelve;
    Mars in four; the Sun, Venus, and Mercury in a year; the moon in
    twenty-eight days. Tush, these are freshmen's suppositions. But
    tell me, hath every sphere a dominion or *intelligentia*?
MEPHISTOPHILIS. Ay.
FAUSTUS. How many heavens, or spheres, are there?

---

[61] "In direction and in time?"

MEPHISTOPHILIS. Nine: the seven planets, the firmament, and the
     empyreal heaven.
FAUSTUS. Well, resolve me in this question: Why have we not
     conjunctions, oppositions, aspects, eclipses, all at one time, but in
     some years we have more, in some less?
MEPHISTOPHILIS. *Per inæqualem motum respectu totius.*[62]
FAUSTUS. Well, I am answered. Tell me who made the world.
MEPHISTOPHILIS. I will not.
FAUSTUS. Sweet Mephistophilis, tell me.
MEPHISTOPHILIS. Move me not, for I will not tell thee.
FAUSTUS. Villain, have I not bound thee to tell me anything?
MEPHISTOPHILIS. Ay, that is not against our kingdom; but this is.
     Think thou on hell, Faustus, for thou art damn'd.
FAUSTUS. Think, Faustus, upon God that made the world.
MEPHISTOPHILIS. Remember this.
FAUSTUS. Ay, go, accursed spirit, to ugly hell.
     'Tis thou hast damn'd distressed Faustus' soul.
     Is't not too late?

     [*Re-enter* GOOD ANGEL *and* EVIL ANGEL.]

EVIL ANGEL. Too late.
GOOD ANGEL. Never too late, if Faustus can repent.
EVIL ANGEL. If thou repent, devils shall tear thee in pieces.
GOOD ANGEL. Repent, and they shall never raze thy skin.

     [*Exeunt* ANGELS.]

FAUSTUS. Ah, Christ, my Saviour,
     Seek to save distressed Faustus' soul.

     [*Enter* LUCIFER, BELZEBUB, *and* MEPHISTOPHILIS.]

LUCIFER. Christ cannot save thy soul, for he is just;
     There's none but I have interest in the same.
FAUSTUS. O, who art thou that look'st so terrible?
LUCIFER. I am Lucifer,
     And this is my companion-prince in hell.
FAUSTUS. O Faustus! they are come to fetch away thy soul!
LUCIFER. We come to tell thee thou dost injure us;
     Thou talk'st of Christ contrary to thy promise;
     Thou should'st not think of God: think of the Devil,
     And of his dam, too.

---

[62] "On account of their unequal motion in relation to the whole."

FAUSTUS. Nor will I henceforth: pardon me in this,
    And Faustus vows never to look to Heaven,
    Never to name God, or to pray to him,
    To burn his Scriptures, slay his ministers,
    And make my spirits pull his churches down.
LUCIFER. Do so, and we will highly gratify thee. Faustus, we are come
    from hell to show thee some pastime. Sit down, and thou shalt see
    all the Seven Deadly Sins appear in their proper shapes.
FAUSTUS. That sight will be as pleasing unto me,
    As Paradise was to Adam the first day
    Of his creation.
LUCIFER. Talk not of Paradise nor creation, but mark this show: talk of
    the Devil, and nothing else.—Come away!

[*Enter the* SEVEN DEADLY SINS.]

Now, Faustus, examine them of their several names and
dispositions.
FAUSTUS. What art thou—the first?
PRIDE. I am Pride. I disdain to have any parents. I am like to Ovid's
    flea: I can creep into every corner of a wench; sometimes, like a
    periwig, I sit upon her brow; or like a fan of feathers, I kiss her
    lips; indeed I do—what do I not? But, fie, what a scent is here! I'll
    not speak another word, except the ground were perfum'd, and
    covered with cloth of arras.
FAUSTUS. What art thou—the second?
COVETOUSNESS. I am Covetousness, begotten of an old churl in an old
    leathern bag; and might I have my wish I would desire that this
    house and all the people in it were turn'd to gold, that I might lock
    you up in my good chest. O, my sweet gold!
FAUSTUS. What art thou—the third?
WRATH. I am Wrath. I had neither father nor mother: I leapt out of a
    lion's mouth when I was scarce half an hour old; and ever since I
    have run up and down the world with this case[63] of rapiers,
    wounding myself when I had nobody to fight withal. I was born in
    hell; and look to it, for some of you shall be my father.
FAUSTUS. What art thou—the fourth?
ENVY. I am Envy, begotten of a chimney sweeper and an oyster-wife. I
    cannot read, and therefore wish all books were burnt. I am lean
    with seeing others eat. O that there would come a famine through
    all the world, that all might die, and I live alone! then thou
    should'st see how fat I would be. But must thou sit and I stand!
    Come down with a vengeance!

---

[63] Pair.

FAUSTUS. Away, envious rascal! What art thou—the fifth?

GLUTTONY. Who, I, sir? I am Gluttony. My parents are all dead, and
the devil a penny they have left me, but a bare pension, and that is
thirty meals a day and ten bevers[64]—a small trifle to suffice nature.
O, I come of a royal parentage! My grandfather was a Gammon of
Bacon, my grandmother a Hogshead of Claret-wine; my godfathers
were these, Peter Pickleherring, and Martin Martlemas-beef.[65] O,
but my godmother, she was a jolly gentlewoman, and well beloved
in every good town and city; her name was Mistress Margery
Marchbeer. Now, Faustus, thou hast heard all my progeny, wilt
thou bid me to supper?

FAUSTUS. No, I'll see thee hanged: thou wilt eat up all my victuals.

GLUTTONY. Then the Devil choke thee!

FAUSTUS. Choke thyself, glutton! Who art thou—the sixth?

SLOTH. I am Sloth. I was begotten on a sunny bank, where I have lain
ever since; and you have done me great injury to bring me from
thence: let me be carried thither again by Gluttony and Lechery.
I'll not speak another word for a king's ransom.

FAUSTUS. What are you, Mistress Minx, the seventh and last?

LECHERY. Who, I, sir? I am one that loves an inch of raw mutton better
than an ell of fried stockfish; and the first letter of my name begins
with Lechery.

LUCIFER. Away to hell, to hell!—Now, Faustus, how dost thou like
this?

[*Exeunt the* SINS.]

FAUSTUS. O, this feeds my soul!

LUCIFER. Tut, Faustus, in hell is all manner of delight.

FAUSTUS. O might I see hell, and return again,
How happy were I then!

LUCIFER. Thou shalt; I will send for thee at midnight.
In meantime take this book; peruse it throughly,
And thou shalt turn thyself into what shape thou wilt.

FAUSTUS. Great thanks, mighty Lucifer!
This will I keep as chary as my life.

LUCIFER. Farewell, Faustus, and think on the Devil.

FAUSTUS. Farewell, great Lucifer! Come, Mephistophilis. [*Exeunt.*]

[*Enter* CHORUS.]

---

[64] Refreshments between meals.

[65] Martlemas or Martinmas was "the customary time for hanging up provisions to
dry which had been salted for the winter."—*Nares.*

CHORUS. Learned Faustus,
   To know the secrets of astronomy,
   Graven in the book of Jove's high firmament,
   Did mount himself to scale Olympus' top,
   Being seated in a chariot burning bright,
   Drawn by the strength of yoky dragons' necks.
   He now is gone to prove cosmography,
   And, as I guess, will first arrive at Rome,
   To see the Pope and manner of his court,
   And take some part of holy Peter's feast,
   That to this day is highly solemnis'd. [*Exit.*]

SCENE VII.

The POPE'S *Privy-chamber.*

[*Enter* FAUSTUS *and* MEPHISTOPHILIS.]

FAUSTUS. Having now, my good Mephistophilis,
   Passed with delight the stately town of Trier,[66]
   Environ'd round with airy mountain-tops,
   With walls of flint, and deep entrenched lakes,
   Not to be won by any conquering prince;
   From Paris next, coasting the realm of France,
   We saw the river Maine fall into Rhine,
   Whose banks are set with groves of fruitful vines;
   Then up to Naples, rich Campania,
   Whose buildings fair and gorgeous to the eye,
   The streets straight forth, and pav'd with finest brick,
   Quarter the town in four equivalents.
   There saw we learned Maro's[67] golden tomb,
   The way he cut, an English mile in length,
   Thorough a rock of stone in one night's space;
   From thence to Venice, Padua, and the rest,
   In one of which a sumptuous temple stands,
   That threats the stars with her aspiring top.
   Thus hitherto has Faustus spent his time:
   But tell me, now, what resting-place is this?
   Hast thou, as erst I did command,
   Conducted me within the walls of Rome?
MEPHISTOPHILIS. Faustus, I have; and because we will not be
   unprovided, I have taken up his Holiness' privy-chamber for our

---

[66] Treves.
[67] Virgil, who was reputed a magician in the Middle Ages, was buried at Naples.

use.

FAUSTUS. I hope his Holiness will bid us welcome.

MEPHISTOPHILIS. Tut, 'tis no matter, man, we'll be bold with his good
    cheer.
    And now, my Faustus, that thou may'st perceive
    What Rome containeth to delight thee with,
    Know that this city stands upon seven hills
    That underprop the groundwork of the same.
    [Just through the midst runs flowing Tiber's stream,
    With winding banks that cut it in two parts:]
    Over the which four stately bridges lean,
    That make safe passage to each part of Rome:
    Upon the bridge called Ponte Angelo
    Erected is a castle passing strong,
    Within whose walls such store of ordnance are,
    And double cannons fram'd of carved brass,
    As match the days within one complete year;
    Besides the gates and high pyramides,
    Which Julius Cæsar brought from Africa.

FAUSTUS. Now by the kingdoms of infernal rule,
    Of Styx, of Acheron, and the fiery lake
    Of ever-burning Phlegethon, I swear
    That I do long to see the monuments
    And situation of bright-splendent Rome:
    Come therefore, let's away.

MEPHISTOPHILIS. Nay, Faustus, stay: I know you'd see the Pope,
    And take some part of holy Peter's feast,
    Where thou shalt see a troop of bald-pate friars,
    Whose *summum bonum* is in belly-cheer.

FAUSTUS. Well, I'm content to compass then some sport,
    And by their folly make us merriment.
    Then charm me, [Mephistophilis,] that I
    May be invisible, to do what I please
    Unseen of any whilst I stay in Rome.

[MEPHISTOPHILIS *charms him.*]

MEPHISTOPHILIS. So, Faustus, now
    Do what thou wilt, thou shalt not be discern'd.

[*Sound a sennett.*[68] *Enter the* POPE *and the* CARDINAL OF LORRAIN
    to the banquet, with FRIARS *attending.*]

---

[68] "A particular set of notes on the trumpet or cornet, different from a flourish."—*Nares.*

POPE. My Lord of Lorrain, wilt please you draw near?

FAUSTUS. Fall to, and the devil choke you an[69] you spare!

POPE. How now! Who's that which spake?—Friars, look about.

FIRST FRIAR. Here's nobody, if it like your Holiness.

POPE. My lord, here is a dainty dish was sent me from the Bishop of Milan.

FAUSTUS. I thank you, sir. [*Snatches the dish.*]

POPE. How now! Who's that which snatched the meat from me? Will no man look? My lord, this dish was sent me from the Cardinal of Florence.

FAUSTUS. You say true; I'll ha't. [*Snatches the dish.*]

POPE. What, again! My lord, I'll drink to your Grace.

FAUSTUS. I'll pledge your Grace. [*Snatches the cup.*]

CARDINAL OF LORRAIN. My lord, it may be some ghost newly crept out of purgatory, come to beg a pardon of your Holiness.

POPE. It may be so. Friars, prepare a dirge to lay the fury of this ghost. Once again, my lord, fall to. [*The* POPE *crosses himself.*]

FAUSTUS. What, are you crossing of yourself?
Well, use that trick no more I would advise you.

[*The* POPE *crosses himself again.*]

Well, there's the second time. Aware the third,
I give you fair warning.

[*The* POPE *crosses himself again, and Faustus hits him a box of the ear; and they all run away.*]

Come on, Mephistophilis, what shall we do?

MEPHISTOPHILIS. Nay, I know not. We shall be curs'd with bell, book, and candle.

FAUSTUS. How! bell, book, and candle,—candle, book, and bell,
Forward and backward to curse Faustus to hell!
Anon you shall hear a hog grunt, a calf bleat, and an ass bray,
Because it is Saint Peter's holiday.

[*Re-enter all the* FRIARS *to sing the Dirge.*]

FIRST FRIAR. Come, brethren, let's about our business with good devotion.

[*They sing.*]

---

[69] If.

Cursed be he that stole away his Holiness' meat from the table!
Maledicat Dominus![70]
Cursed be he that struck his Holiness a blow on the face!
Maledicat Dominus!
Cursed be he that took Friar Sandelo a blow on the pate! *Maledicat
Dominus!*
Cursed be he that disturbeth our holy dirge! *Maledicat Dominus!*
Cursed be he that took away his Holiness' wine! *Maledicat
Dominus! Et omnes sancti!*[71] *Amen!*

[MEPHISTOPHILIS *and* FAUSTUS beat the FRIARS, *and fling
fireworks among them: and so exeunt.*]

[*Enter* CHORUS.]

CHORUS. When Faustus had with pleasure ta'en the view
    Of rarest things, and royal courts of kings,
    He stay'd his course, and so returned home;
    Where such as bear his absence but with grief,
    I mean his friends, and near'st companions,
    Did gratulate his safety with kind words,
    And in their conference of what befell,
    Touching his journey through the world and air,
    They put forth questions of Astrology,
    Which Faustus answer'd with such learned skill,
    As they admir'd and wond'red at his wit.
    Now is his fame spread forth in every land;
    Amongst the rest the Emperor is one,
    Carolus the Fifth, at whose palace now
    Faustus is feasted 'mongst his noblemen.
    What there he did in trial of his art,
    I leave untold—your eyes shall see perform'd. [*Exit.*]

---

[70] "May the Lord curse him."
[71] "And all the saints."

SCENE VIII.

An Inn-yard.

[*Enter* ROBIN *the Ostler with a book in his hand.*]

ROBIN. O, this is admirable! here I ha' stolen one of Dr. Faustus' conjuring books, and i' faith I mean to search come circles for my own use. Now will I make all the maidens in our parish dance at my pleasure, stark naked before me; and so by that means I shall see more than e'er I felt or saw yet.

[*Enter* RALPH *calling* ROBIN.]

RALPH. Robin, prithee come away; there's a gentleman tarries to have his horse, and he would have his things rubb'd and made clean. He keeps such a chafing with my mistress about it; and she has sent me to look thee out; prithee come away.

ROBIN. Keep out, keep out, or else you are blown up; you are dismemb'red, Ralph: keep out, for I am about a roaring piece of work.

RALPH. Come, what dost thou with that same book? Thou canst not read.

ROBIN. Yes, my master and mistress shall find that I can read, he for his forehead, she for her private study; she's born to bear with me, or else my art fails.

RALPH. Why, Robin, what book is that?

ROBIN. What book! Why, the most intolerable book for conjuring that e'er was invented by any brimstone devil.

RALPH. Canst thou conjure with it?

ROBIN. I can do all these things easily with it: first, I can make thee drunk with ippocras[72] at any tabern[73] in Europe for nothing; that's one of my conjuring works.

RALPH. Our Master Parson says that's nothing.

ROBIN. True, Ralph; and more, Ralph, if thou hast any mind to Nan Spit, our kitchenmaid, then turn her and wind her to thy own use as often as thou wilt, and at midnight.

RALPH. O brave Robin, shall I have Nan Spit, and to mine own use? On that condition I'll feed thy devil with horsebread as long as he lives, of free cost.

ROBIN. No more, sweet Ralph: let's go and make clean our boots,

---

[72] Wine mixed with sugar and spices.
[73] Tavern.

which lie foul upon our hands, and then to our conjuring in the
Devil's name. [*Exeunt.*]

SCENE IX.

An Inn.

[*Enter* ROBIN *and* RALPH *with a silver goblet.*]

ROBIN. Come, Ralph, did not I tell thee we were for ever made by this
Doctor Faustus' book? *Ecce signum,*[74] here's a simple purchase[75]
for horsekeepers; our horses shall eat not hay as long as this lasts.

[*Enter the* VINTNER.]

RALPH. But, Robin, here come the vintner.
ROBIN. Hush! I'll gull him supernaturally.
    Drawer, I hope all is paid: God be with you. Come, Ralph.
VINTNER. Soft, sir; a word with you. I must yet have a goblet paid from
    you, ere you go.
ROBIN. I, a goblet, Ralph; I, a goblet! I scorn you, and you are but a,[76]
    &c. I, a goblet! search me.
VINTNER. I mean so, sir, with your favour. [*Searches him.*]
ROBIN. How say you now?
VINTNER. I must say somewhat to your fellow. You, sir!
RALPH. Me, sir! me, sir! search your fill.

[VINTNER *searches him.*]

Now, sir, you may be ashamed to burden honest men with a matter
of truth.
VINTNER. Well, t'one of you hath this goblet about you.
ROBIN. You lie, drawer, 'tis afore me. [*Aside.*] Sirrah you, I'll teach ye
    to impeach honest men;—stand by;—I'll scour you for a goblet!—
    stand aside you had best, I charge you in the name of Belzebub.
    Look to the goblet, Ralph. [*Aside to* RALPH.]
VINTNER. What mean you, sirrah?
ROBIN. I'll tell you what I mean. [*Reads from a book.*]

Sanctobulorum. Periphrasticon—Nay, I'll tickle you, vintner.
    Look to the goblet, Ralph. [*Aside to* RALPH.]

---

[74] "Behold a sign."
[75] Gain.
[76] The abuse was left to the actor's inventiveness.

Polypragmos Belseborams framanto pacostiphos tostu, Mephistophilis, &c. [Reads.]

[*Enter* MEPHISTOPHILIS, *sets squibs at their backs, and then exit. They run about.*]

VINTNER. *O nomine Domini!*[77] what meanest thou, Robin? Thou hast no goblet.

RALPH. *Peccatum peccatorum!*[78] Here's thy goblet, good vintner. [*Gives the goblet to* VINTNER, *who exits.*]

ROBIN. *Misericordia pro nobis!*[79] What shall I do? Good Devil, forgive me now, and I'll never rob thy library more.

[*Re-enter* MEPHISTOPHILIS.]

MEPHISTOPHILIS. Monarch of hell, under whose black survey
Great potentates do kneel with awful fear,
Upon whose altars thousand souls do lie,
How am I vexed with these villains' charms?
From Constantinople am I hither come
Only for pleasure of these damned slaves.

ROBIN. How from Constantinople? You have had a great journey. Will you take sixpence in your purse to pay for you supper, and begone?

MEPHISTOPHILIS. Well, villains, for your presumption, I transform thee into an ape, and thee into a dog; and so begone. [*Exit.*]

ROBIN. How, into an ape? That's brave! I'll have fine sport with the boys. I'll get nuts and apples enow.

RALPH. And I must be a dog.

ROBIN. I'faith thy head will never be out of the pottage pot. [*Exeunt.*]

SCENE X.

The Court of the EMPEROR.

[*Enter* Emperor, FAUSTUS, *and a* KNIGHT *with attendants.*]

EMPEROR. Master Doctor Faustus, I have heard strange report of thy knowledge in the black art, how that none in my empire nor in the whole world can compare with thee for the rare effects of magic; they say thou hast a familiar spirit, by whom thou canst accomplish

---

[77] "In the name of the Lord."
[78] "Sin of sins."
[79] "Mercy on us."

what thou list. This therefore is my request, that thou let me see some proof of thy skill, that mine eyes may be witnesses to confirm what mine ears have heard reported; and here I swear to thee by the honour of mine imperial crown, that, whatever thou doest, thou shalt be no ways prejudiced or endamaged.

KNIGHT. I'faith he looks much like a conjuror. [*Aside.*]

FAUSTUS. My gracious sovereign, though I must confess myself far inferior to the report men have published, and nothing answerable[80] to the honour of your imperial majesty, yet for that love and duty binds me thereunto, I am content to do whatsoever your majesty shall command me.

EMPEROR. Then, Doctor Faustus, mark what I shall say.
>As I was sometime solitary set
>Within my closet, sundry thoughts arose
>About the honour of mine ancestors,
>How they had won by prowess such exploits,
>Got such riches, subdued so many kingdoms
>As we that do succeed, or they that shall
>Hereafter possess our throne, shall
>(I fear me) ne'er attain to that degree
>Of high renown and great authority;
>Amongst which kings is Alexander the Great,
>Chief spectacle of the world's pre-eminence,
>The bright shining of whose glorious acts
>Lightens the world with his[81] reflecting beams,
>As when I heard but motion[82] made of him
>It grieves my soul I never saw the man.
>If therefore thou by cunning of thine art
>Canst raise this man from hollow vaults below,
>Where lies entomb'd this famous conqueror,
>And bring with him his beauteous paramour,
>Both in their right shapes, gesture, and attire
>They us'd to wear during their time of life,
>Thou shalt both satisfy my just desire,
>And give me cause to praise thee whilst I live.

FAUSTUS. My gracious lord, I am ready to accomplish your request so far forth as by art, and power of my Spirit, I am able to perform.

KNIGHT. I'faith that's just nothing at all. [*Aside.*]

FAUSTUS. But, if it like your Grace, it is not in my ability to present before your eyes the true substantial bodies of those two deceased princes, which long since are consumed to dust.

---

[80] Proportionate.
[81] Its.
[82] Mention.

KNIGHT. Ay, marry, Master Doctor, now there's a sign of grace in you, when you will confess the truth. [*Aside.*]

FAUSTUS. But such spirits as can lively resemble Alexander and his paramour shall appear before your Grace in that manner that they [best] live in, in their most flourishing estate; which I doubt not shall sufficiently content your imperial majesty.

EMPEROR. Go to, Master Doctor, let me see them presently.

KNIGHT. Do you hear, Master Doctor? You bring Alexander and his paramour before the Emperor!

FAUSTUS. How then, sir?

KNIGHT. I'faith that's as true as Diana turn'd me to a stag!

FAUSTUS. No, sir, but when Actæon died, he left the horns for you. Mephistophilis, begone.

[*Exit* MEPHISTOPHILIS.]

KNIGHT. Nay, an you go to conjuring. I'll begone. [*Exit.*]

FAUSTUS. I'll meet with you anon for interrupting me so. Here they are, my gracious lord.

[*Re-enter* MEPHISTOPHILIS *with* (SPIRITS *in the shape of*) ALEXANDER *and his* PARAMOUR.]

EMPEROR. Master Doctor, I heard this lady while she liv'd had a wart or mole in her neck: how shall I know whether it be so or no?

FAUSTUS. Your Highness may boldly go and see.

EMPEROR. Sure these are no spirits, but the true substantial bodies of those two deceased princes.

[*Exeunt* SPIRITS.]

FAUSTUS. Will't please your highness now to send for the knight that was so pleasant with me here of late?

EMPEROR. One of you call him forth.

[*Exit* ATTENDANT.]

[*Re-enter the* KNIGHT *with a pair of horns on his head.*]

How now, sir knight! why I had thought thou had'st been a bachelor, but now I see thou hast a wife, that not only gives thee horns, but makes thee wear them. Feel on thy head.

KNIGHT. Thou damned wretch and execrable dog,
Bred in the concave of some monstrous rock,
How darest thou thus abuse a gentleman?

Villain, I say, undo what thou hast done!

FAUSTUS. O, not so fast, sir; there's no haste; but, good, are you rememb'red how you crossed me in my conference with the Emperor? I think I have met with you for it.

EMPEROR. Good Master Doctor, at my entreaty release him; he hath done penance sufficient.

FAUSTUS. My gracious lord, not so much for the injury he off'red me here in your presence, as to delight you with some mirth, hath Faustus worthily requited this injurious knight; which, being all I desire, I am content to release him of his horns: and, sir knight, hereafter speak well of scholars. Mephistophilis, transform him straight.

[MEPHISTOPHILIS *removes the horns.*]

Now, my good lord, having done my duty I humbly take my leave.

EMPEROR. Farewell, Master Doctor; yet, ere you go,
Expect from me a bounteous reward. [*Exeunt.*]

SCENE XI.

A Green; afterwards the House of FAUSTUS.

[*Enter* FAUSTUS *and* MEPHISTOPHILIS.]

FAUSTUS. Now, Mephistophilis, the restless course
That Time doth run with calm and silent foot,
Short'ning my days and thread of vital life,
Calls for the payment of my latest years;
Therefore, sweet Mephistophilis, let us
Make haste to Wittenberg.

MEPHISTOPHILIS. What, will you go on horseback or on foot?

FAUSTUS. Nay, till I'm past this fair and pleasant green, I'll walk on foot.

[*Enter a* HORSE-COURSER.]

HORSE-COURSER. I have been all this day seeking one Master Fustian: mass, see where he is! God save you, Master Doctor!

FAUSTUS. What, horse-courser! You are well met.

HORSE-COURSER. Do you hear, sir? I have brought you forty dollars for your horse.

FAUSTUS. I cannot sell him so: if thou likest him for fifty take him.

HORSE-COURSER. Alas, sir, I have no more.—I pray you speak for me.

MEPHISTOPHILIS. I pray you let him have him: he is an honest fellow, and he has a great charge, neither wife nor child.

FAUSTUS. Well, come, give me your money.

[HORSE-COURSER *gives* FAUSTUS *the money.*]

My boy will deliver him to you. But I must tell you one thing before you have him; ride him not into the water at any hand.

HORSE-COURSER. Why, sir, will he not drink of all waters?

FAUSTUS. O yes, he will drink of all waters, but ride him not into the water: ride him over hedge or ditch, or where thou wilt, but not into the water.

HORSE-COURSER. Well, sir.—Now I am made man for ever. I'll not leave my horse for forty. If he had but the quality of hey-ding-ding, hey-ding-ding, I'd made a brave living on him: he has a buttock as slick as an eel. [*Aside.*] Well, God b' wi' ye, sir, your boy will deliver him me: but hark you, sir; if my horse be sick or ill at ease, if I bring his water to you, you'll tell me what it is.

FAUSTUS. Away, you villain; what, dost think I am a horse-doctor?

[*Exit* HORSE-COURSER.]

What art thou, Faustus, but a man condemn'd to die?
Thy fatal time doth draw to final end;
Despair doth drive distrust unto my thoughts:
Confound these passions with a quiet sleep:
Tush, Christ did call the thief upon the cross;
Then rest thee, Faustus, quiet in conceit. [*Sleeps in his chair.*]

[*Re-enter* HORSE-COURSER, *all wet, crying.*]

HORSE-COURSER. Alas, alas! Doctor Fustian quotha? Mass, Doctor Lopus[83] was never such a doctor. Has given me a purgation has purg'd me of forty dollars; I shall never see them more. But yet, like an ass as I was, I would not be ruled by him, for he bade me I should ride him into no water. Now I, thinking my horse had had some rare quality that he would not have had me known of, I, like a venturous youth rid him into the deep pond at the town's end. I was no sooner in the middle of the pond, but my horse vanished away, and I sat upon a bottle of hay, never so near drowning in my life. But I'll seek out my Doctor, and have my forty dollars again, or I'll make it the dearest horse!—O, yonder is his snipper-

---

[83] Dr. Lopez, physician to Queen Elizabeth, was hanged in 1594 on the charge of conspiring to poison the Queen.

snapper.—Do you hear? You hey-pass,[84] where's your master?

MEPHISTOPHILIS. Why, sir, what would you? You cannot speak with him.

HORSE-COURSER. But I will speak with him.

MEPHISTOPHILIS. Why, he's fast asleep. Come some other time.

HORSE-COURSER. I'll speak with him now, or I'll break his glass windows about his ears.

MEPHISTOPHILIS. I tell thee he has not slept this eight nights.

HORSE-COURSER. An he have not slept this eight weeks, I'll speak with him.

MEPHISTOPHILIS. See where he is, fast asleep.

HORSE-COURSER. Ay, this is he. God save you, Master Doctor! Master Doctor, Master Doctor Fustian!—Forty dollars, forty dollars for a bottle of hay!

MEPHISTOPHILIS. Why, thou seest he hears thee not.

HORSE-COURSER. So ho, ho!—so ho, ho! [*Hollas in his ear.*] No, will you not wake? I'll make you wake ere I go. [*Pulls FAUSTUS by the leg, and pulls it away.*] Alas, I am undone! What shall I do?

FAUSTUS. O my leg, my leg! Help, Mephistophilis! call the officers. My leg, my leg!

MEPHISTOPHILIS. Come, villain, to the constable.

HORSE-COURSER. O lord, sir, let me go, and I'll give you forty dollars more.

MEPHISTOPHILIS. Where be they?

HORSE-COURSER. I have none about me. Come to my ostry[85] and I'll give them you.

MEPHISTOPHILIS. Begone quickly.

[HORSE-COURSER *runs away.*]

FAUSTUS. What, is he gone? Farewell he! Faustus has his leg again, and the horse-courser, I take it, a bottle of hay for his labour. Well, this trick shall cost him forty dollars more.

[*Enter* WAGNER.]

How now, Wagner, what's the news with thee?

WAGNER. Sir, the Duke of Vanholt doth earnestly entreat your company.

FAUSTUS. The Duke of Vanholt! an honourable gentleman, to whom I

---

[84] A juggler's term, like "presto, fly!" Hence applied to the juggler himself.—*Bullen.*

[85] Inn.

must be no niggard of my cunning. Come, Mephistophilis, let's away to him. [*Exeunt.*]

SCENE XII.

The Court of the DUKE OF VANHOLT.

[*Enter the* DUKE (*of* VANHOLT), *the* DUCHESS, FAUSTUS, *and* MEPHISTOPHILIS.]

DUKE. Believe me, Master Doctor, this merriment hath much pleased me.

FAUSTUS. My gracious lord, I am glad it contents you so well.—But it may be, madam, you take no delight in this. I have heard that great-bellied women do long for some dainties or other. What is it, madam? Tell me, and you shall have it.

DUCHESS. Thanks, good Master Doctor; and for I see your courteous intent to pleasure me, I will not hide from you the thing my heart desires; and were it now summer, as it is January and the dead time of the winter, I would desire no better meat than a dish of ripe grapes.

FAUSTUS. Alas, madam, that's nothing! Mephistophilis, begone.

[*Exit* MEPHISTOPHILIS.]

Were it a greater thing than this, so it would content you, you should have it.

[*Re-enter* MEPHISTOPHILIS *with the grapes.*]

Here they be, madam; wilt please you taste on them?

DUKE. Believe me, Master Doctor, this makes me wonder above the rest, that being in the dead time of winter, and in the month of January, how you should come by these grapes.

FAUSTUS. If it like your Grace, the year is divided into two circles over the whole world, that, when it is here winter with us, in the contrary circle it is summer with them, as in India, Saba, and farther countries in the East; and by means of a swift spirit that I have I had them brought hither, as ye see.—How do you like them, madam; be they good?

DUCHESS. Believe me, Master Doctor, they be the best grapes that I e'er tasted in my life before.

FAUSTUS. I am glad they content you so, madam.

DUKE. Come, madam, let us in, where you must well reward this learned man for the great kindness he hath show'd to you.

DUCHESS. And so I will, my lord; and, whilst I live, rest beholding for this courtesy.

FAUSTUS. I humbly thank your Grace.

DUKE. Come, Master Doctor, follow us and receive your reward. [*Exeunt.*]

SCENE XIII.

A room in FAUSTUS' *House.*

[*Enter* WAGNER.]

WAGNER. I think my master shortly means to die,
For he hath given to me all his goods;
And yet, methinks, if that death were so near,
He would not banquet and carouse and swill
Amongst the students, as even now he doth,
Who are at supper with such belly-cheer
As Wagner ne'er beheld in all his life.
See where they come! Belike the feast is ended.

[*Enter* FAUSTUS, *with two or three* SCHOLARS (*and* MEPHISTOPHILIS).]

FIRST SCHOLAR. Master Doctor Faustus, since our conference about fair ladies, which was the beautifullest in all the world, we have determined with ourselves that Helen of Greece was the admirablest lady that ever lived: therefore, Master Doctor, if you will do us that favour, as to let us see that peerless dame of Greece, whom all the world admires for majesty, we should think ourselves much beholding unto you.

FAUSTUS. Gentlemen,
For that I know your friendship is unfeigned,
And Faustus' custom is not to deny
The just requests of those that wish him well,
You shall behold that peerless dame of Greece,
No otherways for pomp and majesty
Than when Sir Paris cross'd the seas with her,
And brought the spoils to rich Dardania.
Be silent, then, for danger is in words.

[*Music sounds, and* HELEN *passeth over the stage.*]

SECOND SCHOLAR. Too simple is my wit to tell her praise,
Whom all the world admires for majesty.

THIRD SCHOLAR. No marvel though the angry Greeks pursued
    With ten years' war the rape of such a queen,
    Whose heavenly beauty passeth all compare.
FIRST SCHOLAR. Since we have seen the pride of Nature's works,
    And only paragon of excellence,
    Let us depart; and for this glorious deed
    Happy and blest be Faustus evermore.
FAUSTUS. Gentlemen, farewell—the same I wish to you.

    [*Exeunt* SCHOLARS *and* WAGNER].

    [*Enter an* OLD MAN.]

OLD MAN. Ah, Doctor Faustus, that I might prevail
    To guide thy steps unto the way of life,
    By which sweet path thou may'st attain the goal
    That shall conduct thee to celestial rest!
    Break heart, drop blood, and mingle it with tears,
    Tears falling from repentant heaviness
    Of thy most vile and loathsome filthiness,
    The stench whereof corrupts the inward soul
    With such flagitious crimes of heinous sins
    As no commiseration may expel,
    But mercy, Faustus, of thy Saviour sweet,
    Whose blood alone must wash away thy guilt.
FAUSTUS. Where art thou, Faustus? Wretch, what hast thou done?
    Damn'd art thou, Faustus, damn'd; despair and die!
    Hell calls for right, and with a roaring voice
    Says "Faustus! come! thine hour is [almost] come!"
    And Faustus [now] will come to do the right.

    [MEPHISTOPHILIS *gives him a dagger.*]

OLD MAN. Ah stay, good Faustus, stay thy desperate steps!
    I see an angel hovers o'er thy head,
    And, with a vial full of precious grace,
    Offers to pour the same into thy soul:
    Then call for mercy, and avoid despair.
FAUSTUS. Ah, my sweet friend, I feel
    Thy words do comfort my distressed soul.
    Leave me a while to ponder on my sins.
OLD MAN. I go, sweet Faustus, but with heavy cheer,
    Fearing the ruin of thy hopeless soul. [*Exit.*]
FAUSTUS. Accursed Faustus, where is mercy now?
    I do repent; and yet I do despair;

Hell strives with grace for conquest in my breast:
What shall I do to shun the snares of death?
MEPHISTOPHILIS. Thou traitor, Faustus, I arrest thy soul
　For disobedience to my sovereign lord;
　Revolt, or I'll in piecemeal tear thy flesh.
FAUSTUS. Sweet Mephistophilis, entreat thy lord
　To pardon my unjust presumption.
　And with my blood again I will confirm
　My former vow I made to Lucifer.
MEPHISTOPHILIS. Do it then quickly, with unfeigned heart,
　Lest greater danger do attend thy drift.

[FAUSTUS *stabs his arm and writes on a paper with his blood.*]

FAUSTUS. Torment, sweet friend, that base and crooked age,[86]
　That durst dissuade me from my Lucifer,
　With greatest torments that our hell affords.
MEPHISTOPHILIS. His faith is great, I cannot touch his soul;
　But what I may afflict his body with
　I will attempt, which is but little worth.
FAUSTUS. One thing, good servant, let me crave of thee,
　To glut the longing of my heart's desire,—
　That I might have unto my paramour
　That heavenly Helen, Which I saw of late,
　Whose sweet embracings may extinguish clean
　These thoughts that do dissuade me from my vow,
　And keep mine oath I made to Lucifer.
MEPHISTOPHILIS. Faustus, this or what else thou shalt desire
　Shall be perform'd in twinkling of an eye.

[*Re-enter* HELEN.]

FAUSTUS. Was this the face that launched a thousand ships
　And burnt the topless[87] towers of Ilium?
　Sweet Helen, make me immortal with a kiss. [*Kisses her.*]
　Her lips suck forth my soul; see where it flies!—
　Come, Helen, come, give me my soul again.
　Here will I dwell, for Heaven is in these lips,
　And all is dross that is not Helena.

[*Enter* OLD MAN.]

---

[86] Old man.
[87] Unsurpassed in height.

I will be Paris, and for love of thee,
Instead of Troy, shall Wittenberg be sack'd;
And I will combat with weak Menelaus,
And wear thy colours on my plumed crest;
Yea, I will wound Achilles in the heel,
And then return to Helen for a kiss.
Oh, thou art fairer than the evening air
Clad in the beauty of a thousand stars;
Brighter art thou than flaming Jupiter
When he appear'd to hapless Semele:
More lovely than the monarch of the sky
In wanton Arethusa's azured arms:
And none but thou shalt be my paramour. [*Exeunt.*]
OLD MAN. Accursed Faustus, miserable man,
That from thy soul exclud'st the grace of Heaven,
And fly'st the throne of his tribunal seat!

[*Enter* DEVILS.]

Satan begins to sift me with his pride:
As in this furnace God shall try my faith,
My faith, vile hell, shall triumph over thee.
Ambitious fiends! see how the heavens smiles
At your repulse, and laughs your state to scorn!
Hence, hell! for hence I fly unto my God.

[*Exeunt on one side* DEVILS, *on the other*, OLD MAN].

SCENE XIV.

The Same.

[*Enter* FAUSTUS *with* SCHOLARS.]

FAUSTUS. Ah, gentlemen!
FIRST SCHOLAR. What ails Faustus?
FAUSTUS. Ah, my sweet chamber-fellow, had I lived with thee, then
    had I lived still! but now I die eternally. Look, comes he not,
    comes he not?
SECOND SCHOLAR. What means Faustus?
THIRD SCHOLAR. Belike he is grown into some sickness by being over
    solitary.
FIRST SCHOLAR. If it be so, we'll have physicians to cure him. 'Tis but
    a surfeit. Never fear, man.
FAUSTUS. A surfeit of deadly sin that hath damn'd both body and soul.

SECOND SCHOLAR. Yet, Faustus, look up to Heaven; remember God's mercies are infinite.

FAUSTUS. But Faustus' offenses can never be pardoned: the serpent that tempted Eve may be sav'd, but not Faustus. Ah, gentlemen, hear me with patience, and tremble not at my speeches! Though my heart pants and quivers to remember that I have been a student here these thirty years, oh, would I had never seen Wittenberg, never read book! And what wonders I have done, All Germany can witness, yea, the world; for which Faustus hath lost both Germany and the world, yea Heaven itself, Heaven, the seat of God, the throne of the blessed, the kingdom of joy; and must remain in hell for ever, hell, ah, hell, for ever! Sweet friends! what shall become of Faustus being in hell for ever?

THIRD SCHOLAR. Yet, Faustus, call on God.

FAUSTUS. On God, whom Faustus hath abjur'd! on God, whom Faustus hath blasphemed! Ah, my God, I would weep, but the Devil draws in my tears. Gush forth blood instead of tears! Yea, life and soul! Oh, he stays my tongue! I would lift up my hands, but see, they hold them, they hold them!

ALL. Who, Faustus?

FAUSTUS. Lucifer and Mephistophilis. Ah, gentlemen, I gave them my soul for my cunning!

ALL. God forbid!

FAUSTUS. God forbade it indeed; but Faustus hath done it. For vain pleasure of twenty-four years hath Faustus lost eternal joy and felicity. I writ them a bill with mine own blood: the date is expired; the time will come, and he will fetch me.

FIRST SCHOLAR. Why did not Faustus tell us of this before, that divines might have pray'd for thee?

FAUSTUS. Oft have I thought to have done so; but the Devil threat'ned to tear me in pieces if I nam'd God; to fetch both body and soul if I once gave ear to divinity: and now 'tis too late. Gentlemen, away! lest you perish with me.

SECOND SCHOLAR. Oh, what shall we do to save Faustus?

FAUSTUS. Talk not of me, but save yourselves, and depart.

THIRD SCHOLAR. God will strengthen me. I will stay with Faustus.

FIRST SCHOLAR. Tempt not God, sweet friend; but let us into the next room, and there pray for him.

FAUSTUS. Ay, pray for me, pray for me! and what noise soever ye hear, come not unto me, for nothing can rescue me.

SECOND SCHOLAR. Pray thou, and we will pray that God may have mercy upon thee.

FAUSTUS. Gentlemen, farewell! If I live till morning I'll visit you: if not—Faustus is gone to hell.

ALL. Faustus, farewell!

[*Exeunt* SCHOLARS. *The clock strikes eleven.*]

FAUSTUS. Ah, Faustus,
    Now hast thou but one bare hour to live,
    And then thou must be damn'd perpetually!
    Stand still, you ever-moving spheres of Heaven,
    That time may cease, and midnight never come;
    Fair Nature's eye, rise, rise again and make
    Perpetual day; or let this hour be but
    A year, a month, a week, a natural day,
    That Faustus may repent and save his soul!
    O lente, lente, curite noctis equi.[88]
    The stars move still,[89] time runs, the clock will strike,
    The Devil will come, and Faustus must be damn'd.
    O, I'll leap up to my God! Who pulls me down?
    See, see where Christ's blood streams in the firmament!
    One drop would save my soul—half a drop: ah, my Christ!
    Ah, rend not my heart for naming of my Christ!
    Yet will I call on him: O spare me, Lucifer!—
    Where is it now? 'Tis gone; and see where God
    Stretcheth out his arm, and bends his ireful brows!
    Mountain and hills come, come and fall on me,
    And hide me from the heavy wrath of God!
    No! no!
    Then will I headlong run into the earth;
    Earth gape! O no, it will not harbour me!
    You stars that reign'd at my nativity,
    Whose influence hath alloted death and hell,
    Now draw up Faustus like a foggy mist
    Into the entrails of yon labouring clouds,
    That when they vomit forth into the air,
    My limbs may issue from their smoky mouths,
    So that my soul may but ascend to Heaven.

[*The watch strikes the half hour*].

    Ah, half the hour is past! 'Twill all be past anon!
    O God!
    If thou wilt not have mercy on my soul,
    Yet for Christ's sake whose blood hath ransom'd me,
    Impose some end to my incessant pain;

---

[88] "Run softly, softly, horses of the night."—Ovid's *Amores*, i, 13.
[89] Without ceasing.

Let Faustus live in hell a thousand years—
A hundred thousand, and—at last—be sav'd!
O, no end is limited to damned souls!
Why wert thou not a creature wanting soul?
Or why is this immortal that thou hast?
Ah, Pythogoras' metempsychosis! were that true,
This soul should fly from me, and I be chang'd
Unto some brutish beast! All beasts are happy,
For when they die,
Their souls are soon dissolv'd in elements;
But mine must live, still to be plagu'd in hell.
Curst be the parents that engend'red me!
No, Faustus: curse thyself: curse Lucifer
That hath depriv'd thee of the joys of Heaven.

[*The clock striketh twelve.*]

O, it strikes, it strikes! Now, body, turn to air,
Or Lucifer will bear thee quick to hell. [*Thunder and lightning.*]
O soul, be chang'd into little water-drops,
And fall into the ocean—ne'er be found.
My God! my God! look not so fierce on me!

[*Enter* DEVILS.]

Adders and serpents, let me breathe awhile!
Ugly hell, gape not! come not, Lucifer!
I'll burn my books!—Ah Mephistophilis!

[*Exeunt* DEVILS *with* FAUSTUS.]

[*Enter* CHORUS.]

CHORUS. Cut is the branch that might have grown full straight,
    And burned is Apollo's laurel bough,
    That sometime grew within this learned man.
    Faustus is gone; regard his hellish fall,
    Whose fiendful fortune may exhort the wise
    Only to wonder at unlawful things,
    Whose deepness doth entice such forward wits
    To practise more than heavenly power permits. [*Exit.*]

DOCTOR FAUSTUS, 1616, THE "B" TEXT

DRAMATIS PERSONAE.

THE POPE.
THE EMPEROR OF GERMANY.
RAYMOND, *king of Hungary.*
DUKE OF SAXONY.
BRUNO.
DUKE OF VANHOLT.
MARTINO, *gentleman.*
FREDERICK, *gentleman.*
BENVOLIO, *gentleman.*
FAUSTUS.
VALDES, *friend to Faustus.*
CORNELIUS, *friend to Faustus.*
WAGNER, *servant to Faustus.*
CLOWN.
ROBIN.
DICK.
VINTNER.
HORSE-COURSER.
CARTER.
AN OLD MAN.
Scholars, Cardinals, Archbishop of Rheims, Bishops, Monks, Friars, Soldiers, and Attendants.

DUCHESS OF VANHOLT.
HOSTESS.

LUCIFER.
BELZEBUB.
MEPHISTOPHILIS.
GOOD ANGEL.
EVIL ANGEL.
THE SEVEN DEADLY SINS.
DEVILS.
Spirits in the shapes of Alexander the Great, of his Paramour, of Darius, and of Helen.

CHORUS.

THE TRAGICAL HISTORY OF DOCTOR FAUSTUS

FROM THE QUARTO OF 1616.

[*Enter* CHORUS.]

CHORUS. Not marching in the fields of Thrasymene,
  Where Mars did mate the warlike Carthagens;[90]
  Nor sporting in the dalliance of love,
  In courts of kings where state is overturn'd;
  Nor in the pomp of proud audacious deeds,
  Intends our Muse to vaunt her[91] heavenly verse:
  Only this, gentles,—we must now perform
  The form of Faustus' fortunes, good or bad:
  And now to patient judgments we appeal,
  And speak for Faustus in his infancy.
  Now is he born of parents base of stock,
  In Germany, within a town call'd Rhodes:
  At riper years, to Wittenberg he went,
  Whereas his kinsmen chiefly brought him up.
  So much he profits in divinity,
  That shortly he was grac'd with doctor's name,
  Excelling all, and sweetly can dispute
  In th' heavenly matters of theology;
  Till swoln with cunning, of[92] a self-conceit,
  His waxen wings did mount above his reach,
  And, melting, heavens conspir'd his overthrow;
  For, falling to a devilish exercise,
  And glutted now with learning's golden gifts,
  He surfeits upon[93] cursed necromancy;
  Nothing so sweet as magic is to him,
  Which he prefers before his chiefest bliss:
  And this the man that in his study sits. [*Exit.*]

[FAUSTUS *discovered in his study.*]

FAUSTUS. Settle thy studies, Faustus, and begin
  To sound the depth of that thou wilt profess:

---

[90] *Carthagens*: So 4tos 1616, 1624, (and compare 4to 1604, p. 79).—2to 1631 "Carthagen." p. 79. (Doctor Faustus, from the quarto of 1604): "Where Mars did mate the Carthaginians;"
[91] *Her*: Old eds. "his."
[92] *Of*: So 4to 1616.—2tos 1624, 1631, "and."
[93] *Upon*: So 4to 1616.—2tos 1624, 1631, "on the."

Having commenc'd, be a divine in show,
Yet level at the end of every art,
And live and die in Aristotle's works.
Sweet Analytics, 'tis thou hast ravish'd me!
Bene disserere et finis logices.
Is, to dispute well, logic's chiefest end?
Affords this art no greater miracle?
Then read no more; thou hast attain'd that end:
A greater subject fitteth Faustus' wit:
Bid Economy farewell, and Galen come:
Be a physician, Faustus; heap up gold,
And be eterniz'd for some wondrous cure:
Summum bonum medicinæ sanitas,
The end of physic is our body's health.
Why, Faustus, hast thou not attain'd that end?
Are not thy bills hung up as monuments,
Whereby whole cities have escap'd the plague,
And thousand[94] desperate maladies been cur'd?
Yet art thou still but Faustus, and a man.
Couldst thou make men to live eternally,
Or, being dead, raise them[95] to life again,
Then this profession were to be esteem'd.
Physic, farewell! Where is Justinian? [*Reads.*]
*Si una eademque res legatur[96] duobus, alter rem, alter valorem rei,
&c.*
A petty[97] case of paltry legacies! [*Reads.*]
Exhæreditare filium non potest pater, nisi, &c.[98]
Such is the subject of the institute,
And universal body of the law:
This study fits a mercenary drudge,
Who aims at nothing but external trash;
Too servile and illiberal for me.
When all is done, divinity is best:
Jerome's Bible, Faustus; view it well. [*Reads.*]

> *Stipendium peccati mors est.* Ha! *Stipendium, &c.* The reward
> of sin is death: that's hard. [*Reads.*] *Si peccasse negamus,
> fallimur, et nulla est in nobis veritas*; If we say that we have
> no sin, we deceive ourselves, and there is no truth in us. Why,
> then, belike we must sin, and so consequently die:
> Ay, we must die an everlasting death.

---

[94] *Thousand:* So 4to 1616.—2tos 1624, 1631, "diuers."

[95] *Them:* So 4to 1616.—2tos 1624, 1631, "men."

[96] *Legatur:* Old eds. "legatus."

[97] *Petty:* I may notice that 4to 1604 has "pretty," which is perhaps the right reading.

[98] *&c.*: So 4tos 1624, 1631.—Not in 4to 1616.

What doctrine call you this, *Che sera, sera,*
What will be, shall be? Divinity, adieu!
These metaphysics of magicians,
And necromantic books are heavenly;
Lines, circles, scenes, letters, and characters;[99]
Ay, these are those that Faustus most desires.
O, what a world of profit and delight,
Of power, of honour, and omnipotence,
Is promis'd to the studious artizan!
All things that move between the quiet poles
Shall be at my command: emperors and kings
Are but obeyed in their several provinces;
But his dominion that exceeds in this,
Stretcheth as far as doth the mind of man;
A sound magician is a demigod:
Here tire, my brains, to gain[100] a deity.

[*Enter* WAGNER.]

Wagner, commend me to my dearest friends,
The German Valdes and Cornelius;
Request them earnestly to visit me.
WAGNER. I will, sir. [*Exit.*]
FAUSTUS. Their conference will be a greater help to me
     Than all my labours, plod I ne'er so fast.

[*Enter* GOOD ANGEL *and* EVIL ANGEL.]

GOOD ANGEL. O, Faustus, lay that damned book aside,
     And gaze not on it, lest it tempt thy soul,
     And heap God's heavy wrath upon thy head!
     Read, read the Scriptures:—that is blasphemy.
EVIL ANGEL. Go forward, Faustus, in that famous art
     Wherein all Nature's treasure is contain'd:
     Be thou on earth as Jove is in the sky,
     Lord and commander of these[101] elements.

-----

[99] *Circles, scenes, letters, and characters*: So 4to 1604 (see note).—The later 4tos
"circles, letters, characters."

Note from (Doctor Faustus, from the quarto of 1604):

"*scenes*: "And sooner may a gulling weather-spie
     By drawing forth heavens *Sceanes* tell certainly," &c.
          Donne's *First Satyre,*—p. 327, ed. 1633."
[100] *Gain*: So 4tos 1624, 1631 (and so 4to 1604).—2to 1616 "get."
[101] *These*: See note.

[*Exeunt* ANGELS.]

FAUSTUS. How am I glutted with conceit of this!
    Shall I make spirits fetch me what I please,
    Resolve me of all ambiguities,
    Perform what desperate enterprise[102] I will?
    I'll have them fly to India for gold,
    Ransack the ocean for orient pearl,
    And search all corners of the new-found world
    For pleasant fruits and princely delicates;
    I'll have them read me strange philosophy,
    And tell the secrets of all foreign kings;
    I'll have them wall all Germany with brass,
    And make swift Rhine circle fair[103] Wittenberg;
    I'll have them fill the public schools with silk,[104]
    Wherewith the students shall be bravely clad;
    I'll levy soldiers with the coin they bring,
    And chase the Prince of Parma from our land,
    And reign sole king of all the provinces;
    Yea, stranger engines for the brunt of war,
    Than was the fiery keel at Antwerp-bridge,
    I'll make my servile spirits to invent.

[*Enter* VALDES *and* CORNELIUS.]

    Come, German Valdes, and Cornelius,
    And make me blest[105] with your sage conference.
    Valdes, sweet Valdes, and Cornelius,
    Know that your words have won me at the last
    To practice magic and concealed arts.
    Philosophy is odious and obscure;
    Both law and physic are for petty wits:
    'Tis magic, magic that hath ravish'd me.
    Then, gentle friends, aid me in this attempt;

Note from (Doctor Faustus, from the quarto of 1604):

"*These elements*: So again, "Within the bowels of *these* elements," &c., on p. 18, first col,—"*these*" being equivalent to *the*. (Not unfrequently in our old writers *these* is little more than redundant.)"

[102] *Enterprise*: So 4to 1616.—2tos 1624, 1631, "enterprises."

[103] *Make swift Rhine circle fair*: So 4to 1616.—2tos 1624, 1631, "with *swift Rhine circle* all."

[104] *Silk*: Old eds. "skill."

[105] *Blest*: So 4to 1616.—2tos 1624, 1631, "wise."

And I, that have with subtle syllogisms
Gravell'd the pastors of the German church,
And made the flowering pride of Wittenberg
Swarm[106] to my problems, as th' infernal spirits
On sweet Musæus when he came to hell,
Will be as cunning as Agrippa was,
Whose shadow made all Europe honour him.

VALDES. Faustus, these books, thy wit, and our experience,
Shall make all nations to[107] canonize us.
As Indian Moors obey their Spanish lords,
So shall the spirits of every element
Be always serviceable to us three;
Like lions shall they guard us when we please;
Like Almain rutters with their horsemen's staves,
Or Lapland giants, trotting by our sides;
Sometimes like women, or unwedded maids,
Shadowing more beauty in their airy brows
Than have[108] the white breasts of the queen of love:
From Venice shall they[109] drag huge[110] argosies,
And from America the golden fleece
That yearly stuffs[111] old Philip's treasury;
If learned Faustus will be resolute.

FAUSTUS. Valdes, as resolute am I in this
As thou to live: therefore object it not.

CORNELIUS. The miracles that magic will perform
Will make thee vow to study nothing else.
He that is grounded in astrology,
Enrich'd with tongues, well seen in minerals,
Hath all the principles magic doth require:
Then doubt not, Faustus, but to be renowm'd,[112]

---

[106] *Swarm*: So 4tos 1624, 1631.—2to 1616 "Sworne."
[107] *To*: So 4to 1616.—Not in 4tos 1624, 1631.
[108] *Have*: So 4tos 1624, 1631.—2to 1616 "has."
[109] *Shall they*: So 4to 1616.—2tos 1624, 1631, "they shall."
[110] *Huge*: So 4to 1616.—2tos 1624, 1631, "whole."
[111] *Stuffs*: So 4tos 1624, 1631.—2to 1616 "stuff'd."
[112] *Renowm'd*: So 4to 1616 (See note).—2tos 1624, 1631, "renown'd."

Note from (The First Part of Tamburlaine the Great):

"*Renowmèd*: i.e. renowned.—So the 8vo.—The 4to "renowned."—The form "*renowmed*" (Fr. *renommé*) occurs repeatedly afterwards in this play, according to the 8vo. It is occasionally found in writers posterior to Marlowe's time. e.g.

"Of Constantines great towne *renoum'd* in vaine."
Verses to King James, prefixed to Lord Stirling's
Monarchicke Tragedies, ed. 1607."

And more frequented for this mystery
Than heretofore the Delphian oracle.
The spirits tell me they can dry the sea,
And fetch the treasure of all foreign wrecks,
Yea, all the wealth that our forefathers hid
Within the massy entrails of the earth:
Then tell me, Faustus, what shall we three want?
FAUSTUS. Nothing, Cornelius. O, this cheers my soul!
Come, shew me some demonstrations magical,
That I may conjure in some bushy grove,
And have these joys in full possession.
VALDES. Then haste thee to some solitary grove,
And bear wise Bacon's and Albertus'[113] works,
The Hebrew Psalter, and New Testament;
And whatsoever else is requisite
We will inform thee ere our conference cease.
CORNELIUS. Valdes, first let him know the words of art;
And then, all other ceremonies learn'd,
Faustus may try his cunning by himself.
VALDES. First I'll instruct thee in the rudiments,
And then wilt thou be perfecter than I.
FAUSTUS. Then come and dine with me, and, after meat,
We'll canvass every quiddity thereof;
For, ere I sleep, I'll try what I can do:
This night I'll conjure, though I die therefore. [*Exeunt.*]

[*Enter* TWO SCHOLARS.]

FIRST SCHOLAR. I wonder what's become of Faustus, that was wont to
make our schools ring with *sic probo*.
SECOND SCHOLAR. That shall we presently know; here comes his boy.

[*Enter* WAGNER.]

FIRST SCHOLAR. How now, sirrah! where's thy master?
WAGNER. God in heaven knows.
SECOND SCHOLAR. Why, dost not thou know, then?
WAGNER. Yes, I know; but that follows not.
FIRST SCHOLAR. Go to, sirrah! leave your jesting, and tell us where he
is.
WAGNER. That follows not by force of argument, which you, being
licentiates, should stand upon: therefore acknowledge your error,
and be attentive.

---

[113] *Albertus'*: Old eds. "Albanus."

SECOND SCHOLAR. Then you will not tell us?

WAGNER. You are deceived, for I will tell you: yet, if you were not dunces, you would never ask me such a question; for is he not *corpus naturale*? and is not that mobile? then wherefore should you ask me such a question? But that I am by nature phlegmatic, slow to wrath, and prone to lechery (to love, I would say), it were not for you to come within forty foot of the place of execution, although I do not doubt but to see you both hanged the next sessions. Thus having triumphed over you, I will set my countenance like a precisian, and begin to speak thus:—Truly, my dear brethren, my master is within at dinner, with Valdes and Cornelius, as this wine, if it could speak, would inform your worships: and so, the Lord bless you, preserve you, and keep you, my dear brethren! [*Exit.*]

FIRST SCHOLAR. O Faustus!
　　Then I fear that which I have long suspected,
　　That thou art fallen into that[114] damned art
　　For which they two are infamous through the world.

SECOND SCHOLAR. Were he a stranger, not allied to me,
　　The danger of his soul would make me mourn.
　　But, come, let us go and inform the Rector:
　　It may be his grave counsel may reclaim him.[115]

FIRST SCHOLAR. I fear me nothing will reclaim him now.

SECOND SCHOLAR. Yet let us see what we can do. [*Exeunt.*]

[*Enter* FAUSTUS.[116]]

FAUSTUS. Now that the gloomy shadow of the night,
　　Longing to view Orion's drizzling look,
　　Leaps from th' antarctic world unto the sky,
　　And dims the welkin with her[117] pitchy breath,
　　Faustus, begin thine incantations,
　　And try if devils will obey thy hest,
　　Seeing thou hast pray'd and sacrific'd to them.
　　Within this circle is Jehovah's name,
　　Forward and backward anagrammatis'd,
　　Th' abbreviated names of holy saints,
　　Figures of every adjunct to the heavens,
　　And characters of signs and erring[118] stars,

---

[114] *That*: So 4tos 1616, 1624.—2to 1631 "the."

[115] *Him*: So 4to 1616.—Not in 4tos 1624, 1631.

[116] *Enter Faustus*: Old eds. "*Thunder. Enter Lucifer and 4 deuils, Faustus to them with this speech,*"—wrongly.

[117] *Her*: So 4to 1616.—2tos 1624, 1631, "his."

[118] *Erring*: So 4tos 1624, 1631.—2to 1616 "euening."

By which the spirits are enforc'd to rise:
Then fear not, Faustus, to be resolute,
And try the utmost magic can perform. [*Thunder.*]
Sint mihi dii Acherontis propitii! Valeat numen triplex Jehovoe!
Ignei, aerii, aquatani spiritus, salvete! Orientis princeps Belzebub,
inferni ardentis monarcha, et Demogorgon, propitiamus vos, ut
appareat et surgat Mephistophilis Dragon, quod tumeraris:[119] *per*
Jehovam, Gehennam, et consecratam aquam quam nunc spargo,
signumque crucis quod nunc facio, et per vota nostra, ipse nunc
surgat nobis dicatus [120]*Mephistophilis!*

[*Enter* MEPHISTOPHILIS.]

I charge thee to return, and change thy shape;
Thou art too ugly to attend on me:
Go, and return an old Franciscan friar;
That holy shape becomes a devil best.

[*Exit* MEPHISTOPHILIS.]

I see there's virtue in my heavenly words.
Who would not be proficient in this art?
How pliant is this Mephistophilis,
Full of obedience and humility!
Such is the force of magic and my spells.

[*Re-enter* MEPHISTOPHILIS *like a Franciscan friar.*]

MEPHISTOPHILIS. Now, Faustus, what wouldst thou have me do?
FAUSTUS. I charge thee wait upon me whilst I live,
To do whatever Faustus shall command,
Be it to make the moon drop from her sphere,
Or the ocean to overwhelm the world.

---

[119] *Mephistophilis Dragon, quod tumeraris*: See note.

Note from (Doctor Faustus, from the quarto of 1604):

"*Surgat Mephistophilis, quod tumeraris*: The later 4tos have "*surgat Mephistophilis*
Dragon, *quod tumeraris*."—There is a corruption here, which seems to defy emendation.
For "*quod* tumeraris," Mr. J. Crossley, of Manchester, would read (rejecting the word
"*Dragon*") "*quòd* tu mandares" (the construction being "*quod tu mandares ut
Mephistophilis appareat et surgat*"): but the "*tu*" does not agree with the preceding
"*vos*."—The Revd. J. Mitford proposes "*surgat Mephistophilis, per Dragon* (or *Dagon*)
quod numen est äcris.""

[120] *Dicatus*: So 4tos 1624, 1631.—2to 1616 "dicatis."

MEPHISTOPHILIS. I am a servant to great Lucifer,
    And may not follow thee without his leave:
    No more than he commands must we perform.
FAUSTUS. Did not he charge thee to appear to me?
MEPHISTOPHILIS. No, I came hither[121] of mine own accord.
FAUSTUS. Did not my conjuring speeches[122] raise thee? speak!
MEPHISTOPHILIS. That was the cause, but yet *per accidens*;[123]
    For, when we hear one rack the name of God,
    Abjure the Scriptures and his Saviour Christ,
    We fly, in hope to get his glorious soul;
    Nor will we come, unless he use such means
    Whereby he is in danger to be damn'd.
    Therefore the shortest cut for conjuring
    Is stoutly to abjure all godliness,
    And pray devoutly to the prince of hell.
FAUSTUS. So Faustus hath
    Already done; and holds this principle,
    There is no chief but only Belzebub;
    To whom Faustus doth dedicate himself.
    This word "damnation" terrifies not me,
    For I confound hell in Elysium:
    My ghost be with the old philosophers!
    But, leaving these vain trifles of men's souls,
    Tell me what is that Lucifer thy lord?
MEPHISTOPHILIS. Arch-regent and commander of all spirits.
FAUSTUS. Was not that Lucifer an angel once?
MEPHISTOPHILIS. Yes, Faustus, and most dearly lov'd of God.
FAUSTUS. How comes it, then, that he is prince of devils?
MEPHISTOPHILIS. O, by aspiring pride and insolence;
    For which God threw him from the face of heaven.
FAUSTUS. And what are you that live with Lucifer?
MEPHISTOPHILIS. Unhappy spirits that fell[124] with Lucifer,
    Conspir'd against our God with Lucifer,
    And are for ever damn'd with Lucifer.
FAUSTUS. Where are you damn'd?
MEPHISTOPHILIS. In hell.
FAUSTUS. How comes it, then, that thou art out of hell?
MEPHISTOPHILIS. Why, this is hell, nor am I out of it:
    Think'st thou that I, that saw the face of God,
    And tasted the eternal joys of heaven,
    Am not tormented with ten thousand hells,

---

[121] *Came hither*: So 4tos 1624, 1631.—2to 1616 "*came* now *hether*."
[122] *Speeches*: So 4to 1604.—Not in the later 4tos.
[123] *Accidens*: So 4tos 1624, 1631.—2to 1616 "accident."
[124] *Fell*: So 4to 1604.—The later 4tos "liue."

In being depriv'd of everlasting bliss?
O, Faustus, leave these frivolous demands,
Which strike[125] a terror to my fainting soul!
FAUSTUS. What, is great Mephistophilis so passionate
For being deprived of the joys of heaven?
Learn thou of Faustus manly fortitude,
And scorn those joys thou never shalt possess.
Go bear these tidings to great Lucifer:
Seeing Faustus hath incurr'd eternal death
By desperate thoughts against Jove's deity,
Say, he surrenders up to him his soul,
So he will spare him four and twenty years,
Letting him live in all voluptuousness;
Having thee ever to attend on me,
To give me whatsoever I shall ask,
To tell me whatsoever I demand,
To slay mine enemies, and to aid my friends,
And always be obedient to my will.
Go, and return to mighty Lucifer,
And meet me in my study at midnight,
And then resolve me of thy master's mind.
MEPHISTOPHILIS. I will, Faustus. [*Exit.*]
FAUSTUS. Had I as many souls as there be stars,
I'd give them all for Mephistophilis.
By him I'll be great emperor of the world,
And make a bridge thorough[126] the moving air,
To pass the ocean with a band of men;
I'll join the hills that bind the Afric shore,
And make that country continent to Spain,
And both contributary to my crown:
The Emperor shall not live but by my leave,
Nor any potentate of Germany.
Now that I have obtain'd what I desir'd,
I'll live in speculation of this art,
Till Mephistophilis return again. [*Exit.*]

[*Enter* WAGNER *and* CLOWN.]

WAGNER. Come hither, sirrah boy.
CLOWN. Boy! O, disgrace to my person! zounds, boy in your face!
You have seen many boys with beards, I am sure.
WAGNER. Sirrah,[127] hast thou no comings in?

---

[125] *Strike*: So 4to 1631.—2tos 1616, 1624, "strikes."
[126] *Thorough*: So 4to 1631.—2tos 1616, 1624, "through."

CLOWN. Yes, and goings out too, you may see, sir.

WAGNER. Alas, poor slave! see how poverty jests in his nakedness! I know the villain's out of service, and so hungry, that I know he would give his soul to the devil for a shoulder of mutton, though it were blood-raw.

CLOWN. Not so neither: I had need to have it well roasted, and good sauce to it, if I pay so dear, I can tell you.

WAGNER. Sirrah, wilt thou be my man, and wait on me, and I will make thee go like *Qui mihi discipulus*?

CLOWN. What, in verse?

WAGNER. No, slave; in beaten silk and staves-acre.

CLOWN. Staves-acre! that's good to kill vermin: then, belike, if I serve you, I shall be lousy.

WAGNER. Why, so thou shalt be, whether thou dost it or no; for, sirrah, if thou dost not presently bind thyself to me for seven years, I'll turn all the lice about thee into familiars, and make them tear thee in pieces.

CLOWN. Nay, sir, you may save[128] yourself a labour, for they are as familiar with me as if they paid for their meat and drink, I can tell you.

WAGNER. Well, sirrah, leave your jesting, and take these guilders. [*Gives money.*]

CLOWN. Yes, marry, sir; and I thank you too.

WAGNER. So, now thou art to be at an hour's warning, whensoever and wheresoever the devil shall fetch thee.

CLOWN. Here, take your guilders again;[129] I'll none of 'em.

WAGNER. Not I; thou art pressed: prepare thyself, or[130] I will presently raise up two devils to carry thee away.—Banio! Belcher!

CLOWN. Belcher! an Belcher come here, I'll belch him: I am not afraid of a devil.

[*Enter two* DEVILS.]

WAGNER. How now, sir! will you serve me now?

CLOWN. Ay, good Wagner; take away the devil[s], then.

WAGNER. Spirits, away!

[*Exeunt* DEVILS.]

Now, sirrah, follow me.

---

[127] *Sirrah*: So 4to 1616.—Not in 4tos 1624, 1631.
[128] *Save*: So 4tos 1616, 1624.—2to 1631 "spare."
[129] *Again*: So 4tos 1624, 1631.—Not in 4to 1616.
[130] *Or*: Old eds. "for."

CLOWN. I will, sir: but hark you, master; will you teach me this conjuring occupation?

WAGNER. Ay, sirrah, I'll teach thee to turn thyself to a dog, or a cat, or a mouse, or a rat, or any thing.

CLOWN. A dog, or a cat, or a mouse, or a rat!

O, brave, Wagner!

WAGNER. Villain, call me Master Wagner, and see that you walk attentively, and let your right eye be always diametrally fixed upon my left heel, that thou mayst *quasi vestigiis nostris*[131] *insistere.*

CLOWN. Well, sir, I warrant you. [*Exeunt.*]

[FAUSTUS *discovered in his study.*]

FAUSTUS. Now, Faustus,
    Must thou needs be damn'd, canst thou not be sav'd.
    What boots it, then, to think on God or heaven?
    Away with such vain fancies, and despair;
    Despair in God, and trust in Belzebub:
    Now, go not backward,[132] Faustus; be resolute:
    Why[133] waver'st thou? O, something soundeth in mine ear,
    "Abjure this magic, turn to God again!"
    Why, he loves thee not;
    The god thou serv'st is thine own appetite,
    Wherein is fix'd the love of Belzebub:
    To him I'll build an altar and a church,
    And offer lukewarm blood of new-born babes.

[*Enter* GOOD ANGEL *and* EVIL ANGEL.]

EVIL ANGEL. Go forward, Faustus, in that famous[134] art.

GOOD ANGEL. Sweet Faustus, leave that execrable art.

FAUSTUS. Contrition, prayer, repentance—what of[135] these?

GOOD ANGEL. O, they are means to bring thee unto heaven!

EVIL ANGEL. Rather illusions, fruits of lunacy,
    That make men[136] foolish that do use them most.

GOOD ANGEL. Sweet Faustus, think of heaven and heavenly things.

EVIL ANGEL. No, Faustus; think of honour and of wealth.

[*Exeunt* ANGELS.]

---

[131] *Vestigiis Nostris*: Old eds. "vestigias nostras."

[132] *Backward*: So 4to 1616 (and so 4to 1604).—2tos 1624, 1631, "backe."

[133] *Why*: So 4to 1616 (and so 4to 1604).—Not in 4tos 1624, 1631.

[134] *That famous*: So 4to 1616.—2tos 1624, 1631, "that *most* famous."

[135] *Of*: So 4to 1616.—2tos 1624, 1631, "be."

[136] *Men*: So 4tos 1624, 1631 (and so 4to 1604).—2to 1616 "them."

FAUSTUS. Wealth!
   Why, the signiory of Embden shall be mine.
   When Mephistophilis shall stand by me,
   What power can hurt me? Faustus, thou art safe:
   Cast no more doubts.—Mephistophilis, come,
   And bring glad tidings from great Lucifer;—
   Is't not midnight?—come Mephistophilis,
   And bring glad tidings from great Lucifer;—
   Is't not midnight?—come Mephistophilis,
   Veni, veni, Mephistophile![137]

   [*Enter* MEPHISTOPHILIS.]

   Now tell me what saith Lucifer, thy lord?
MEPHISTOPHILIS. That I shall wait on Faustus whilst he lives,
   So he will buy my service with his soul.
FAUSTUS. Already Faustus hath hazarded that for thee.
MEPHISTOPHILIS. But now thou must bequeath it solemnly,
   And write a deed of gift with thine own blood;
   For that security craves Lucifer.
   If thou deny it, I must back to hell.
FAUSTUS. Stay, Mephistophilis, and tell me, what good will my soul do
   thy lord?
MEPHISTOPHILIS. Enlarge his kingdom.
FAUSTUS. Is that the reason why he tempts us thus?
MEPHISTOPHILIS. *Solamen miseris socios habuisse doloris.*
FAUSTUS. Why, have you any pain that torture others?
MEPHISTOPHILIS. As great as have the human souls of men.
   But, tell me, Faustus, shall I have thy soul?
   And I will be thy slave, and wait on thee,
   And give thee more than thou hast wit to ask.
FAUSTUS. Ay, Mephistophilis, I'll give it thee.[138]
MEPHISTOPHILIS. Then, Faustus, stab thine[139] arm courageously,
   And bind thy soul, that at some certain day
   Great Lucifer may claim it as his own;
   And[140] then be thou as great as Lucifer.
FAUSTUS. [*Stabbing his arm*] Lo, Mephistophilis, for love of thee,
   Faustus hath cut his arm, and with his proper blood
   Assures his soul to be great Lucifer's,
   Chief lord and regent of perpetual night!

---

[137] *Mephistophile*: So 4to 1616.—2tos 1624, 1631, "Mephostophilis."
[138] *Thee*: So 4to 1604.—The later 4tos "him."
[139] *Thine*: So 4tos 1624, 1631.—2to 1616 "thy."
[140] *And*: So 4to 1616.—Not in 4tos 1624, 1631.

View here this blood that trickles from mine arm,
And let it be propitious for my[141] wish.
MEPHISTOPHILIS. But, Faustus,
Write it in manner of a deed of gift.
FAUSTUS. [*Writing*] Ay, so I do. But, Mephistophilis,
My blood congeals, and I can write no more.
MEPHISTOPHILIS. I'll fetch thee fire to dissolve it straight. [*Exit.*]
FAUSTUS. What might the staying of my blood portend?
Is it[142] unwilling I should write this bill?
Why streams it not, that I may write afresh?
Faustus gives to thee his soul: O, there it stay'd!
Why shouldst thou not? is not thy soul thine own?
Then write again, *Faustus gives to thee his soul.*[143]

[*Re-enter* MEPHISTOPHILIS *with the chafer of fire.*]

MEPHISTOPHILIS. See, Faustus, here is fire; set it on.
FAUSTUS. So, now the blood begins to clear again;
Now will I make an[144] end immediately. [*Writes.*]
MEPHISTOPHILIS. What will not I do to obtain his soul? [*Aside.*]
FAUSTUS. *Consummatum est*; this bill is ended,
And Faustus hath bequeath'd his soul to Lucifer.
But what is this inscription on mine arm?
Homo, fuge: whither should[145] I fly?
If unto God,[146] he'll throw me down to hell.
My senses are deceiv'd; here's nothing writ:—
O, yes, I see it plain; even here is writ,
Homo, fuge: yet shall not Faustus fly.
MEPHISTOPHILIS. I'll fetch him somewhat to delight his mind. [*Aside, and then exit.*]

[*Enter* DEVILS, *giving crowns and rich apparel to* FAUSTUS. *They dance, and then depart.*]

[*Re-enter* MEPHISTOPHILIS.]

FAUSTUS. What means this show? speak, Mephistophilis.
MEPHISTOPHILIS. Nothing, Faustus, but to delight thy mind,
And let thee see what magic can perform.

[141] *My*: So 4to 1616.—2tos 1624, 1631, "thy."
[142] *Is it*: So 4to 1616.—2tos 1624, 1631, "It is."
[143] *Soul*: So 4to 1616.—Not in 4tos 1624, 1631.
[144] *An*: So 4tos 1616, 1631.—Not in 4to 1624.
[145] *Should*: So 4tos 1616, 1624.—2to 1631 "shall."
[146] *God*: So 4to 1604.—The later 4tos "heauen."

FAUSTUS. But may I raise such spirits when I please?
MEPHISTOPHILIS. Ay, Faustus, and do greater things than these.
FAUSTUS. Then, Mephistophilis, receive this scroll,[147]
    A deed of gift of body and of soul:
    But yet conditionally that thou perform
    All covenants and articles between us both!
MEPHISTOPHILIS. Faustus, I swear by hell and Lucifer
    To effect all promises between us both!
FAUSTUS. Then hear me read it, Mephistophilis. [*Reads.*]
    On these conditions following. First, that Faustus may be a spirit
    in form and substance. Secondly, that Mephistophilis shall be his
    servant, and be by him commanded. Thirdly, that Mephistophilis
    shall do for him, and bring him whatsoever he desires.[148] *Fourthly,*
    that he shall be in his chamber or house invisible. Lastly, that he
    shall appear to the said John Faustus, at all times, in what shape
    and form soever he please. I, John Faustus, of Wittenberg, doctor,
    by these presents, do give both body and soul to Lucifer prince of
    the east, and his minister Mephistophilis; and furthermore grant
    unto them, that, four-and-twenty years being expired, and these
    articles above-written being inviolate, full power to fetch or carry
    the said John Faustus, body and soul, flesh and[149] *blood, into their*
    habitation wheresoever. By me, John Faustus.
MEPHISTOPHILIS. Speak, Faustus, do you deliver this as your deed?
FAUSTUS. Ay, take it, and the devil give thee good of it!
MEPHISTOPHILIS. So, now, Faustus, ask me what thou wilt.
FAUSTUS. First I will question with[150] thee about hell.
    Tell me, where is the[151] place that men call hell?
MEPHISTOPHILIS. Under the heavens.
FAUSTUS. Ay, so are all things else; but whereabouts?
MEPHISTOPHILIS. Within the bowels of these elements,
    Where we are tortur'd and remain for ever:
    Hell hath no limits, nor is circumscrib'd
    In one self-place; but where we are is hell,

---

[147] *This scroll*: So 4to 1616.—Not in 4tos 1624, 1631.
[148] *He desires*: Not in the 4tos. See note.

Note from (Doctor Faustus, from the quarto of 1604):

"He desires: Not in any of the four 4tos. In the tract just cited, i.e. *The History of Doctor Faustus*, ed. 1648. The "3d Article" stands thus,—"That Mephostophiles should bring him any thing, and doe for him whatsoever." Sig. A 4, ed. 1648. A later ed. adds "he desired." Marlowe, no doubt, followed some edition of the HISTORY in which these words, or something equivalent to them, had been omitted by mistake. (2to 1661, which I consider as of no authority, has "he requireth.")"

[149] *And*: So 4tos 1624, 1631.—Not in 4to 1616.
[150] *With*: So 4to 1604.—Not in the later 4tos.
[151] *The*: So 4to 1616.—2tos 1624, 1631, "that."

And where hell is, there must we ever be:
And, to be short, when all the world dissolves,
And every creature shall be purified,
All places shall be hell that are[152] not heaven.
FAUSTUS. I think hell's a fable.[153]
MEPHISTOPHILIS. Ay, think so still, till experience change thy mind.
FAUSTUS. Why, dost thou think that Faustus shall be damn'd?
MEPHISTOPHILIS. Ay, of necessity, for here's the scroll
    In which thou hast given thy soul to Lucifer.
FAUSTUS. Ay, and body too; and what of that?
    Think'st thou that Faustus is so fond to imagine
    That, after this life, there is any pain?
    No, these are trifles and mere old wives' tales.
MEPHISTOPHILIS. But I am an instance to prove the contrary,
    For I tell thee I am damn'd and now in hell.
FAUSTUS. Nay, an this be hell, I'll willingly be damn'd:
    What! sleeping, eating, walking, and disputing!
    But, leaving this, let me have a wife,
    The fairest maid in Germany;
    For I am wanton and lascivious,
    And cannot live without a wife.
MEPHISTOPHILIS. Well, Faustus, thou shalt have a wife.

[MEPHISTOPHILIS *fetches in a* WOMAN-DEVIL.]

FAUSTUS. What sight is this?
MEPHISTOPHILIS. Now, Faustus, wilt thou have a wife?
FAUSTUS. Here's a hot whore, indeed: no, I'll no wife.
MEPHISTOPHILIS. Marriage is but a ceremonial toy,
    And, if thou lov'st me, think no more of it.
    I'll cull thee out the fairest courtezans,
    And bring them every morning to thy bed:
    She whom thine[154] eye shall like, thy[155] heart shall have,
    Were she as chaste as was[156] Penelope,
    As wise as Saba, or as beautiful
    As was bright Lucifer before his fall.
    Here, take this book, peruse it well:
    The iterating of these lines brings gold;
    The framing of this circle on the ground
    Brings thunder, whirlwinds, storm, and lightning;

---

[152] *Are*: So 4tos 1624, 1631.—2to 1616 "is."
[153] *Hell's a fable*: So 4to 1616.—2tos 1624, 1631, "hell's a MEERE fable."
[154] *Thine*: So 4tos 1616, 1624.—2to 1631 "thy."
[155] *Thy*: So 4tos 1616, 1631.—2to 1624 "thine."
[156] *Was*: So 4to 1616.—2tos 1624, 1631, "were."

Pronounce this thrice devoutly to thyself,
And men in harness[157] shall appear to thee,
Ready to execute what thou command'st.
FAUSTUS. Thanks, Mephistophilis, for this sweet book:
This will I keep as chary as my life. [*Exeunt.*]

[*Enter* FAUSTUS, *in his study, and* MEPHISTOPHILIS.]

FAUSTUS. When I behold the heavens,[158] then I repent,

---

[157] *Harness*: i.e. armour.
[158] *This will I keep as chary as my life.* [*Exeunt.*]

[*Enter* FAUSTUS, *in his study, and* MEPHISTOPHILIS.]

FAUSTUS. *When I behold the heavens, &c.*: Old eds. (that is, 4tos 1616, 1624, 1631) thus;
"This will I keepe, as chary as my life. [*Exeunt.*]

[*Enter* WAGNER *solus.*]

WAGNER. Learned Faustus
    To know the secrets of Astronomy
    Grauen in the booke of Joues high firmament,
    Did mount himselfe to scale Olympus top,
    Being seated in a chariot burning bright,
    Drawne by the strength of yoaky [2to 1624 "yoaked": Dragons necks,
    He now is gone to proue Cosmography,
    And as I gesse will first arriue at Rome,
    To see the Pope and manner of his Court;
    And take some part of holy Peters feast,
    That to [2tos 1624, 1631, "on": this day is highly solemnized.

[*Exit* WAGNER.]

[*Enter* FAUSTUS *in his Study, and* MEPHISTOPHILIS.]

FAUSTUS. When I behold the heauens," &c.

The lines which I have here omitted belong to a subsequent part of the play, where
they will be found with considerable additions, and are rightly assigned to the *Chorus*.
(As given in the present place by the 4tos 1616, 1624, 1631, these lines exhibit the text of
the earlier *Faustus*; see note 1.) It would seem that something was intended to intervene
here between the exit of Faustus and Mephistophilis, and their re-appearance on the
stage: compare, however, the preceding play, see note 2.

Note 1 from (Doctor Faustus, from the quarto of 1604):

"FAUSTUS. Great thanks, mighty Lucifer!
    This will I keep as chary as my life.
LUCIFER. Farewell, Faustus, and think on the devil.
FAUSTUS. Farewell, great Lucifer.

[*Exeunt* LUCIFER *and* BELZEBUB.]

And curse thee, wicked Mephistophilis,
Because thou hast depriv'd me of those joys.
MEPHISTOPHILIS. 'Twas thine[159] own seeking, Faustus; thank thyself.
But, think'st thou heaven is[160] such a glorious thing?
I tell thee, Faustus, it is not half so fair
As thou, or any man that breathes[161] on earth.
FAUSTUS. How prov'st thou that?
MEPHISTOPHILIS. 'Twas made for man; then he's more excellent.
FAUSTUS. If heaven was made for man, 'twas made for me:
I will renounce this magic and repent.

[*Enter* GOOD ANGEL *and* EVIL ANGEL.]

Come, Mephistophilis. [*Exeunt.*]

[*Enter* CHORUS.]

CHORUS. Learned Faustus,
To know the secrets of astronomy
Graven in the book of Jove's high firmament,
Did mount himself to scale Olympus' top,
Being seated in a chariot burning bright,
Drawn by the strength of yoky dragons' necks.
He now is gone to prove cosmography,
And, as I guess, will first arrive at Rome,
To see the Pope and manner of his court,
And take some part of holy Peter's feast,
That to this day is highly solemniz'd. [*Exit.*]

[*Enter* FAUSTUS *and* MEPHISTOPHILIS.]

FAUSTUS. Having now, my good Mephistophilis,
Pass'd with delight the stately town of Trier," etc.

Note 2 from (Doctor Faustus, from the quarto of 1604):

"RALPH. O, brave, Robin! shall I have Nan Spit, and to mine own use? On that
CONDITION I'll feed thy devil with horse-bread as long as he lives, of free
cost.
ROBIN. No more, sweet Ralph: let's go and make clean our boots, which lie foul
upon our hands, and then to our conjuring in the devil's name. [*Exeunt.*]

[*Enter* ROBIN and RALPH *with a silver goblet.*]

ROBIN. Come, Ralph: did not I tell thee, we were for ever made by this Doctor
Faustus' book? *ecce, signum*! here's a simple purchase for horse-keepers: our
horses shall eat no hay as long as this lasts.
RALPH. But, Robin, here comes the Vintner."

[159] *Thine*: So 4tos 1616, 1624.—2to 1631 "thy."
[160] *Is*: So 4to 1616.—Not in 4tos 1624, 1631.
[161] *Breathes*: So 4tos 1624, 1631.—2to 1616 "breathe."

GOOD ANGEL. Faustus, repent; yet God will pity thee.
EVIL ANGEL. Thou art a spirit; God cannot pity thee.
FAUSTUS. Who buzzeth in mine ears[162] I am a spirit?
    Be I a devil, yet God may pity me;
    Yea, God will pity me, if I repent.
EVIL ANGEL. Ay, but Faustus never shall repent.

    [*Exeunt* ANGELS.]

FAUSTUS. My heart is harden'd, I cannot repent;
    Scarce can I name salvation, faith, or heaven:
    Swords, poisons, halters, and envenom'd steel
    Are laid before me to despatch myself;
    And long ere this I[163] should have done the deed,
    Had not sweet pleasure conquer'd deep despair.
    Have not I made blind Homer sing to me
    Of Alexander's love and Œnon's death?
    And hath not he, that built the walls of Thebes
    With ravishing sound of his melodious harp,
    Made music with my Mephistophilis?
    Why should I die, then, or basely despair?
    I am resolv'd; Faustus shall not repent.—
    Come, Mephistophilis, let us dispute again,
    And reason of divine astrology.
    Speak, are there many spheres above the moon?
    Are all celestial bodies but one globe,
    As is the substance of this centric earth?
MEPHISTOPHILIS. As are the elements, such are the heavens,
    Even from the moon unto th' empyreal orb,
    Mutually folded in each other's spheres,
    And jointly move upon one axletree,
    Whose termine[164] is term'd the world's wide pole;
    Nor are the names of Saturn, Mars, or Jupiter
    Feign'd, but are erring[165] stars.
FAUSTUS. But have they all one motion, both *situ et tempore*?

---

[162] *Ears*: So 4tos 1616, 1631.—2to 1624 "eare."

[163] *This* I: So 4tos 1616, 1631.—2to 1624 "*this* time *I*."

[164] *Termine*: I may notice that 4to 1604 (see note.) has "terminine," which at least is better for the metre.

Note from (Doctor Faustus, from the quarto of 1604):

"Whose terminine is term'd the world's wide pole;"

[165] *Erring*: So 4to 1604.—The later 4tos "euening."

MEPHISTOPHILIS. All move from east to west in four-and-twenty hours upon the poles of the world; but differ in their motions upon the poles of the zodiac.

FAUSTUS. These slender questions Wagner can decide:
Hath Mephistophilis no greater skill?
Who knows not the double motion[166] of the planets?
That the first is finish'd in a natural day;
The second thus; Saturn in thirty years; Jupiter in twelve;
Mars in four; the Sun, Venus, and Mercury in a year; the Moon in twenty-eight days. These are freshmen's questions. But tell me, hath every sphere a dominion or *intelligentia*?

MEPHISTOPHILIS. Ay.

FAUSTUS. How many heavens or spheres are there?

MEPHISTOPHILIS. Nine; the seven planets, the firmament, and the empyreal heaven.

FAUSTUS. But is there not *cælum igneum et crystallinum*?

MEPHISTOPHILIS. No, Faustus, they be but fables.

FAUSTUS. Resolve me, then, in this one question; why are not conjunctions, oppositions, aspects, eclipses, all at one time, but in some years we have more, in some less?

MEPHISTOPHILIS. *Per inæqualem motum respectu totius.*

FAUSTUS. Well, I am answered. Now tell me who made the world?

MEPHISTOPHILIS. I will not.

FAUSTUS. Sweet Mephistophilis, tell me.

MEPHISTOPHILIS. Move me not, Faustus.

FAUSTUS. Villain, have I not bound thee to tell me any thing?

MEPHISTOPHILIS. Ay,[167] that is not against our kingdom; this is.
Thou art damned; think thou of hell.

FAUSTUS. Think, Faustus, upon God that made the world.

MEPHISTOPHILIS. Remember this. [*Exit.*]

FAUSTUS. Ay, go, accursed spirit, to ugly hell!
'Tis thou hast damn'd distressed Faustus' soul.
Is't not too late?

[*Re-enter* GOOD ANGEL *and* EVIL ANGEL.]

EVIL ANGEL. Too late.

GOOD ANGEL. Never too late, if Faustus will repent.

EVIL ANGEL. If thou repent, devils will tear thee in pieces.

GOOD ANGEL. Repent, and they shall never raze thy skin.

[*Exeunt* ANGELS.]

---

[166] *Motion*: So 4tos 1616, 1631.—2to 1624 "motions."
[167] *Ay*: So 4to 1616.—Not in 4tos 1624, 1631.

FAUSTUS. O Christ, my Saviour, my Saviour
Help to save distressed Faustus' soul!

[*Enter* LUCIFER, BELZEBUB, *and* MEPHISTOPHILIS.]

LUCIFER. Christ cannot save thy soul, for he is just:
    There's none but I have interest in the same.
FAUSTUS. O, what art thou that look'st so terribly?
LUCIFER. I am Lucifer,
    And this is my companion-prince in hell.
FAUSTUS. O Faustus, they are come to fetch thy soul!
BELZEBUB. We are come to tell thee thou dost injure us.
LUCIFER. Thou call'st of Christ, contrary to thy promise.
BELZEBUB. Thou shouldst not think on God.
LUCIFER. Think of the devil.
BELZEBUB. And his dam too.
FAUSTUS. Nor will Faustus henceforth: pardon him for this,
    And Faustus vows never to look to heaven.
LUCIFER. So shalt thou shew thyself an obedient servant,
    And we will highly gratify thee for it.
BELZEBUB. Faustus, we are come from hell in person to shew thee
    some pastime: sit down, and thou shalt behold the Seven Deadly
    Sins appear to thee in their own proper shapes and likeness.
FAUSTUS. That sight will be as pleasant unto me,
    As Paradise was to Adam the first day
    Of his creation.
LUCIFER. Talk not of Paradise or creation; but mark the show.—
    Go, Mephistophilis, and[168] fetch them in.

[MEPHISTOPHILIS *brings in the* SEVEN DEADLY SINS.]

BELZEBUB. Now, Faustus, question them of their names and
    dispositions.
FAUSTUS. That shall I soon.—What art thou, the[169] first?
PRIDE. I am Pride. I disdain to have any parents. I am like to Ovid's
    flea; I can creep into every corner of a wench; sometimes, like a
    perriwig, I sit upon her brow; next, like a necklace, I hang about
    her neck; then, like a fan of feathers, I kiss her lips;[170] and then,
    turning myself to a wrought smock, do what I list. But, fie, what a

---

[168] *And*: So 4to 1631.—Not in 4tos 1616, 1624.
[169] *The*: So 4tos 1616, 1631.—Not in 4to 1624.
[170] *Lips*: So 4to 1604.—Not in the later 4tos.

smell is here! I'll not speak a word more for a king's ransom, unless the ground be perfumed, and covered with cloth of arras.

FAUSTUS. Thou art a proud knave, indeed.—What art thou, the second?

COVETOUSNESS. I am Covetousness, begotten of an old churl, in a leather bag: and, might I now obtain my wish, this house, you, and all, should turn to gold, that I might lock you safe into my chest: O my sweet gold!

FAUSTUS. And what art thou, the third?

ENVY. I am Envy, begotten of a chimney-sweeper and an oyster-wife. I cannot read, and therefore wish all books burned. I am lean with seeing others eat. O, that there would come a famine over all the world, that all might die, and I live alone! then thou shouldst see how fat I'd be. But must thou sit, and I stand? come down, with a vengeance!

FAUSTUS. Out, envious wretch!—But what art thou, the fourth?

WRATH. I am Wrath. I had neither father nor mother: I leapt out of a lion's mouth when I was scarce an hour old; and ever since have run[171] up and down the world with this[172] case of rapiers, wounding myself when I could get none to fight withal. I was born in hell; and look to it, for some of you shall be my father.

FAUSTUS. And what art thou, the fifth?

GLUTTONY. I am Gluttony. My parents are all dead, and the devil a penny they have left me, but a small pension, and that buys me thirty meals a-day and ten bevers,—a small trifle to suffice nature. I come[173] of a royal pedigree: my father was a Gammon of Bacon, my mother was a Hogshead of Claret-wine; my godfathers were these, Peter Pickled-herring and Martin Martlemas-beef; but my godmother, O, she was an ancient gentlewoman; her name was Margery March-beer. Now, Faustus, thou hast heard all my progeny; wilt thou bid me to supper?

FAUSTUS. Not I.

GLUTTONY. Then the devil choke thee!

FAUSTUS. Choke thyself, glutton!—What art thou, the sixth?

SLOTH. Heigho! I am Sloth. I was begotten on a sunny bank.
Heigho! I'll not speak a word more for a king's ransom.

FAUSTUS. And what are you, Mistress Minx, the seventh and last?

LECHERY. Who, I,[174] sir? I am one that loves an inch of raw mutton better than an ell of fried stock-fish; and the first letter of my name begins with L.[175]

---

[171] *And ever since have run*: So 4to 1616.—2tos 1624, 1631, "and *haue euer since* run."
[172] *This*: So 4to 1604.—The later 4tos "these."
[173] *Come*: So 4to 1616.—2tos 1624, 1631, "came."
[174] *I*: So 4tos 1624, 1631.—2to 1616 "I I."
[175] *L*: Old eds. "Lechery." See note.

Note from (Doctor Faustus, from the quarto of 1604):

LUCIFER. Away to hell, away! On, piper!

[*Exeunt the* SINS.]

FAUSTUS. O, how this sight doth delight my soul!
LUCIFER. Tut,[176] Faustus, in hell is all manner of delight.
FAUSTUS. O, might I see hell, and return again safe,
    How happy were I then!
LUCIFER. Faustus, thou shalt; at midnight I will send for thee.
    Meanwhile peruse this book and view it throughly,
    And thou shalt turn thyself into what shape thou wilt.
FAUSTUS. Thanks, mighty Lucifer!
    This will I keep as chary as my life.
LUCIFER. Now, Faustus, farewell.
FAUSTUS. Farewell, great Lucifer.

[*Exeunt* LUCIFER *and* BELZEBUB.]

Come, Mephistophilis. [*Exeunt.*]

[*Enter* ROBIN,[177] *with a book.*]

ROBIN. What, Dick! look to the horses there, till I come again. I have
    gotten one of Doctor Faustus' conjuring-books; and now we'll
    have such knavery as't passes.

[*Enter* DICK.]

DICK. What, Robin! you must come away and walk the horses.
ROBIN. I walk the horses! I scorn't, faith:[178] I have other matters in
    hand: let the horses walk themselves, an they will.—[*Reads.*] *A per
    se, a*; *t, h, e, the*; *o per se, o*; *Demy orgon gorgon.*—Keep further
    from me, O thou illiterate and unlearned hostler!
DICK. 'Snails, what hast thou got there? a book! why, thou canst not
    tell[179] ne'er a word on't.
ROBIN. That thou shalt see presently: keep out of the circle,

---

"L.: All the 4tos "Lechery."—Here I have made the alteration recommended by Mr.
Collier in his Preface to *Coleridge's Seven Lectures on Shakespeare and Milton*, p. cviii."

[176] *Tut*: So 4to 1604.—The later 4tos "But."

[177] *Robin*: Old eds. "the Clowne" (and so frequently afterwards): but he is evidently
a distinct person from the "Clown," Wagner's attendant, who has previously appeared
(see p. 12). Most probably the parts of the Clown and Robin were played by the same
actor; and hence the confusion in the old eds.

[178] *Faith*: So 4to 1616.—2tos 1624, 1631 "i'faith." (And so afterwards in this scene.)

[179] *Not tell*: So 4to 1616.—Not in 4tos 1624, 1631.

I say, lest I send you into the ostry with a vengeance.

DICK. That's like, faith! you had best leave your foolery; for, an my master come, he'll conjure you, faith.

ROBIN. My master conjure me! I'll tell thee what; an my master come here, I'll clap as fair a[180] pair of horns on's head as e'er thou sawest in thy life.

DICK. Thou need'st[181] not do that, for my mistress hath done it.

ROBIN. Ay, there be of us here that have waded as deep into matters as other men, if they were disposed to talk.

DICK. A plague take you! I thought you did not sneak up and down after her for nothing. But, I prithee, tell me in good sadness, Robin, is that a conjuring-book?

ROBIN. Do but speak what thou'lt have me to do, and I'll do't: if thou'lt dance naked, put off thy clothes, and I'll conjure thee about presently; or, if thou'lt go but to the tavern with me, I'll give thee white wine, red wine, claret-wine, sack, muscadine, malmsey, and whippincrust, hold, belly, hold;[182] and we'll not pay one penny for it.

DICK. O, brave! Prithee,[183] let's to it presently, for I am as dry as a dog.

ROBIN. Come, then, let's away. [*Exeunt.*]

[*Enter* CHORUS.]

CHORUS. Learned Faustus,
    To find the secrets of astronomy
    Graven in the book of Jove's high firmament,
    Did mount him[184] up to scale Olympus' top;
    Where, sitting in a chariot burning bright,
    Drawn by the strength of yoked dragons' necks,
    He views[185] the clouds, the planets, and the stars,
    The tropic zones, and quarters of the sky,
    From the bright circle of the horned moon
    Even to the height of *Primum Mobile*;
    And, whirling round with this[186] circumference,
    Within the concave compass of the pole,
    From east to west his dragons swiftly glide,
    And in eight days did bring him home again.
    Not long he stay'd within his quiet house,

---

[180] *As fair a*: So 4to 1616.—2tos 1624, 1631, "a faire."

[181] *Need'st*: So 4tos 1616, 1624.—2to 1631 "needs."

[182] *Hold, belly, hold*: Compare Florio's *Dict.*, 1611; "*Iosa, Good Store*, hold-bellie-hold."

[183] *Prithee*: So 4to 1616.—2tos 1624, 1631, "I prithee."

[184] *Him*: So 4tos 1616, 1624.—Not in 4to 1631.

[185] *He views*: So 4to 1616.—2tos 1624, 1631, "To view."

[186] *With this*: So 4tos 1616, 1631.—2to 1624 "with *his*." This passage is sufficiently obscure.

To rest his bones after his weary toil;
But new exploits do hale him out again:
And, mounted then upon a dragon's back,
That with his wings did part the subtle air,
He now is gone to prove cosmography,
That measures coasts and kingdoms of the earth;
And, as I guess, will first arrive at Rome,
To see the Pope and manner of his court,
And take some part of holy Peter's feast,
The which this day is highly solemniz'd. [*Exit.*]

[*Enter* FAUSTUS *and* MEPHISTOPHILIS.]

FAUSTUS. Having now, my good Mephistophilis,
Pass'd with delight the stately town of Trier,
Environ'd round[187] with airy mountain-tops,
With walls of flint, and deep-entrenched lakes,
Not to be won by any conquering prince;
From Paris next, coasting the realm of France,
We saw the river Maine fall into Rhine,[188]
Whose banks are set with groves of fruitful vines;
Then up to[189] Naples, rich Campania,
Whose buildings fair and gorgeous to the eye,
The streets straight forth, and pav'd with finest brick,
Quarter the town in four equivalents:[190]
There saw we learned Maro's golden tomb;
The way he cut, an English mile in length,
Thorough[191] a rock of stone, in one night's space;
From thence to Venice, Padua, and the rest,[192]
In one of which a sumptuous temple stands,
That threats the stars with her aspiring top,
Whose frame is pav'd with sundry-colour'd stones,
And roof'd aloft with curious work in gold.
Thus hitherto hath Faustus spent his time:
But tell me[193] now, what resting-place is this?
Hast thou, as erst I did command,
Conducted me within the walls of Rome?
MEPHISTOPHILIS. I have, my Faustus; and, for proof thereof,

---

[187] *Round*: So 4to 1616.—Not in 4tos 1624, 1631.
[188] *Rhine*: So 4tos 1624, 1631.—2to 1616 "Rhines."
[189] *Up to*: So 4to 1616.—2tos 1624, 1631, "vnto."
[190] *Quarter the town in four equivalents*: So 4to 1604.—Not in the later 4tos.
[191] *Thorough*: so 4to 1631.—2tos 1616, 1624, "Through."
[192] *Rest*: So 4to 1604.—The later 4tos "East."
[193] *Me*: So 4tos 1616, 1631.—Not in 4to 1624.

This is the goodly palace of the Pope;
And, 'cause we are no common guests,
I choose his privy-chamber for our use.
FAUSTUS. I hope his Holiness will bid us[194] welcome.
MEPHISTOPHILIS. All's one, for we'll be bold with his venison.
But now, my Faustus, that thou mayst perceive
What Rome contains for to delight thine eyes,
Know that this city stands upon seven hills
That underprop the groundwork of the same:
Just through[195] the midst runs flowing Tiber's stream,
With winding banks that cut it in two parts;
Over the which two stately bridges lean,
That make safe passage to each part of Rome:
Upon the bridge call'd Ponte[196] Angelo
Erected is a castle passing strong,
Where thou shalt see such store of ordnance,
As that the double cannons, forg'd of brass,
Do match[197] the number of the days contain'd
Within the compass of one complete year;
Beside the gates, and high pyramides,
That Julius Caesar brought from Africa.
FAUSTUS. Now, by the kingdoms of infernal rule,
Of Styx, of Acheron, and the fiery lake
Of ever-burning Phlegethon, I swear
That I do long to see the[198] monuments
And situation of bright-splendent Rome:
Come, therefore, let's away.
MEPHISTOPHILIS. Nay, stay, my Faustus: I know you'd see the Pope,
And take some part of holy Peter's feast,
The which, in state and[199] high solemnity,
This day, is held through Rome and Italy,
In honour of the Pope's triumphant victory.
FAUSTUS. Sweet Mephistophilis, thou pleasest me.
Whilst I am here on earth, let me be cloy'd
With all things that delight the heart of man:
My four-and-twenty years of liberty
I'll spend in pleasure and in dalliance,
That Faustus' name, whilst[200] this bright frame doth stand,

---

[194] *Us*: So 4to 1616.—2tos 1624, 1631, "you."
[195] *Through*: So 4tos 1616, 1624.—2to 1631 "thorow."
[196] *Ponte*: Old eds. "Ponto."
[197] *Match*: So 4tos 1624, 1631.—2to 1616 "watch."
[198] *The*: so 4to 1616.—2tos 1624, 1631, "those."
[199] *In state and*: So 4tos 1624, 1631.—2to 1616 "this day with."
[200] *Whilst*: So 4to 1616.—2tos 1624, 1631, "while."

May be admir'd thorough[201] the furthest land.

MEPHISTOPHILIS. 'Tis well said, Faustus. Come, then, stand by me,
    And thou shalt see them come immediately.

FAUSTUS. Nay, stay, my gentle Mephistophilis,
    And grant me my[202] request, and then I go.
    Thou know'st, within the compass of eight days
    We view'd the face of heaven, of earth, and hell;
    So high our dragons soar'd into the air,
    That, looking down, the earth appear'd to me
    No bigger than my hand in quantity;
    There did we view the kingdoms of the world,
    And what might please mine eye I there beheld.
    Then in this show let me an actor be,
    That this proud Pope may Faustus' cunning[203] see.

MEPHISTOPHILIS. Let it be so, my Faustus. But, first, stay,
    And view their triumphs as they pass this way;
    And then devise what best contents thy mind,
    By cunning in thine art to cross the Pope,
    Or dash the pride of this[204] solemnity;
    To make his monks and abbots stand like apes,
    And point like antics at[205] his triple crown;
    To beat the beads about the friars' pates,
    Or clap huge horns upon the Cardinals' heads;
    Or any villany thou canst devise;
        And I'll perform it,[206] Faustus. Hark! they come:
    This day shall make thee be admir'd in Rome.

[*Enter the* CARDINALS *and* BISHOPS, *some bearing crosiers, some
    the pillars;* MONKS *and* FRIARS, *singing their procession; then
    the* POPE, RAYMOND *King of Hungary, the* ARCHBISHOP OF
    RHEIMS, BRUNO *led in chains, and* ATTENDANTS.]

POPE. Cast down our footstool.

RAYMOND. Saxon Bruno, stoop,
    Whilst on thy back his Holiness ascends
    Saint Peter's chair and state pontifical.

BRUNO. Proud Lucifer, that state belongs to me;
    But thus I fall to Peter, not to thee.

---

[201] *Thorough*: So 4to 1631.—2tos 1616, 1624, "through."

[202] *My*: Qy. "one"?

[203] *Cunning*: So 4tos 1624, 1631.—2to 1616 "comming." (And so in the fourth line
of the next speech.)

[204] *This*: So 4to 1616.—2tos 1624, 1631, "his."

[205] *At*: So 4to 1616.—2tos 1624, 1631, "to."

[206] *It*: So 4to 1616.—Not in 4tos 1624, 1631.

POPE. To me and Peter shalt thou grovelling lie,
    And crouch before the Papal dignity.—
    Sound trumpets, then; for thus Saint Peter's heir,
    From Bruno's back, ascends Saint Peter's chair.

[*A flourish while he ascends.*]

    Thus, as the gods creep on with feet of wool,
    Long ere with iron hands they punish men,
    So shall our sleeping vengeance now arise,
    And smite with death thy hated enterprise.[207]—
    Lord Cardinals of France and Padua,
    Go forthwith to our[208] holy consistory,
    And read, amongst the statutes decretal,
    What, by the holy council held at Trent,
    The sacred synod hath decreed for him
    That doth assume the Papal government
    Without election and a true consent:
    Away, and bring us word with speed.
CARDINAL OF FRANCE. We go, my lord.

[*Exeunt* CARDINALS *of France and Padua.*]

POPE. Lord Raymond.

[*They converse in dumb show.*]

FAUSTUS. Go, haste thee, gentle Mephistophilis,
    Follow the cardinals to the consistory;
    And, as they turn their superstitious books,
    Strike them with sloth and drowsy idleness,
    And make them sleep so sound, that in their shapes
    Thyself and I may parley with this[209] Pope,
    This proud confronter of the Emperor;
    And, in despite of all his holiness,
    Restore this Bruno to his liberty,
    And bear him to the states of Germany.
MEPHISTOPHILIS. Faustus, I go.
FAUSTUS. Despatch it soon:
    The Pope shall curse, that Faustus came to Rome.

---

[207] *And smite with death thy hated enterprise*: So 4to 1616.—Not in 4tos 1624, 1631.
[208] *Our*: So 4to 1616.—2tos 1624, 1631, "the."
[209] *This*: So 4to 1616.—2tos 1624, 1631, "the."

[*Exeunt* FAUSTUS *and* MEPHISTOPHILIS.]

BRUNO. Pope Adrian, let me have right[210] of law:
    I was elected by the Emperor.
POPE. We will depose the Emperor for that deed,
    And curse the people that submit to him:
    Both he and thou shall[211] stand excommunicate,
    And interdict from church's privilege
    And all society of holy men.
    He grows too proud in his authority,
    Lifting his lofty head above the clouds,
    And, like a steeple, overpeers the church:
    But we'll pull down his haughty insolence;
    And, as Pope Alexander, our progenitor,
    Trod on the neck of German Frederick,
    Adding this golden sentence to our praise,
    "That Peter's heirs should tread on Emperors,
    And walk upon the dreadful adder's back,
    Treading the lion and the dragon down,
    And fearless spurn the killing basilisk,"
    So will we quell that haughty schismatic,
    And, by authority apostolical,
    Depose him from his regal government.
BRUNO. Pope Julius swore to princely Sigismond,
    For him and the succeeding Popes of Rome,
    To hold the Emperors their lawful lords.
POPE. Pope Julius did abuse the church's rights,
    And therefore none of his decrees can stand.
    Is not all power on earth bestow'd on us?
    And therefore, though we would, we cannot err.
    Behold this silver belt, whereto is fix'd
    Seven golden seals, fast sealed with seven seals,
    In token of our seven-fold power from heaven,
    To bind or loose, lock fast, condemn or judge,
    Resign or seal, or what so pleaseth us:
    Then he and thou, and all the world, shall stoop,
    Or be assured of our dreadful curse,
    To light as heavy as the pains of hell.

[*Re-enter* FAUSTUS *and* MEPHISTOPHILIS, *in the shapes of the* CARDINALS *of France and Padua.*]

---

[210] *Have right*: So 4tos 1624, 1631.—2to 1616 "haue *some* right."
[211] *Shall*: So 4tos 1624, 1631.—2to 1616 "shalt."

MEPHISTOPHILIS. Now tell me, Faustus, are we not fitted well?

FAUSTUS. Yes, Mephistophilis; and two such cardinals
 Ne'er serv'd a holy Pope as we shall do.
 But, whilst they sleep within the consistory,
 Let us salute his reverend fatherhood.

RAYMOND. Behold, my lord, the Cardinals are return'd.

POPE. Welcome, grave fathers: answer presently
 What hath[212] our holy council there decreed
 Concerning Bruno and the Emperor,
 In quittance of their late conspiracy
 Against our state and papal dignity?

FAUSTUS. Most sacred patron of the church of Rome,
 By full consent of all the synod[213]
 Of priests and prelates, it is thus decreed,—
 That Bruno and the German Emperor
 Be held as Lollards and bold schismatics,
 And proud disturbers of the church's peace;
 And if that Bruno, by his own assent,
 Without enforcement of the German peers,
 Did seek to wear the triple diadem,
 And by your death to climb Saint Peter's chair,
 The statutes decretal have thus decreed,—
 He shall be straight condemn'd of heresy,
 And on a pile of faggots burnt to death.

POPE. It is enough. Here, take him to your charge,
 And bear him straight to Ponte[214] Angelo,
 And in the strongest tower enclose him fast.
 To-morrow, sitting in our consistory,
 With all our college of grave cardinals,
 We will determine of his life or death.
 Here, take his[215] triple crown along with you,
 And leave it in the church's treasury.
 Make haste again, my good Lord Cardinals,
 And take our blessing apostolical.

MEPHISTOPHILIS. So, so; was never devil thus bless'd before.

FAUSTUS. Away, sweet Mephistophilis, be gone;
 The Cardinals will be plagu'd for this anon.

[*Exeunt* FAUSTUS *and* MEPHISTOPHILIS *with* BRUNO.]

---

[212] *Hath*: So 4tos 1624, 1631.—2to 1616 "haue."

[213] *Synod*: Qy. "*Holy* synod"?

[214] *Ponte*: Old eds. "Ponto."

[215] *His*: So 4to 1616.—2tos 1624, 1631, "this."

POPE. Go presently and bring a banquet forth,
  That we may solemnize Saint Peter's feast,
  And with Lord Raymond, King of Hungary,
  Drink to our late and happy victory.

[*A Sennet*[216] *while the banquet is brought in; and then enter*
  FAUSTUS *and* MEPHISTOPHILIS *in their own shapes.*]

MEPHISTOPHILIS. Now, Faustus, come, prepare thyself for mirth:
  The sleepy Cardinals are hard at hand,
  To censure Bruno, that is posted hence,
  And on a proud-pac'd steed, as swift as thought,
  Flies o'er the Alps to fruitful Germany,
  There to salute the woful Emperor.
FAUSTUS. The Pope will curse them for their sloth to-day,
  That slept both Bruno and his crown away.
  But now, that Faustus may delight his mind,
  And by their folly make some merriment,
  Sweet Mephistophilis, so charm me here,
  That I may walk invisible to all,
  And do whate'er I please, unseen of any.
MEPHISTOPHILIS. Faustus, thou shalt: then kneel down presently,
  Whilst on thy head I lay my hand,
  And charm thee with this magic wand.
  First, wear this girdle; then appear
  Invisible to all are here:
  The planets seven, the gloomy air,
  Hell, and the Furies' forked hair,
  Pluto's blue fire, and Hecat's tree,
  With magic spells so compass thee,
  That no eye may thy body see!
  So, Faustus, now, for all their holiness,
  Do what thou wilt, thou shalt not be discern'd.
FAUSTUS. Thanks, Mephistophilis.—Now, friars, take heed,
  Lest Faustus make your shaven crowns to bleed.
MEPHISTOPHILIS. Faustus, no more: see, where the Cardinals come!

[*Re-enter the* CARDINALS *of France and* PADUA *with a book.*]

---

[216] *Sennet*: Old eds. "Senit" and "Sonet". See note.

Note from (Doctor Faustus, from the quarto of 1604):

  "*Sonnet*: Variously written, *Sennet, Signet, Signate,* &c.—A particular set of notes
on the trumpet, or cornet, different from a flourish. See Nares's *Gloss.* in V. *Sennet.*"

POPE. Welcome, Lord Cardinals; come, sit down.—
    Lord Raymond, take your seat.—Friars, attend,
    And see that all things be[217] in readiness,
    As best beseems this solemn festival.
CARDINAL OF FRANCE. First, may it please your sacred Holiness
    To view the sentence of the reverend synod
    Concerning Bruno and the Emperor?
POPE. What needs this question? did I not tell you,
    To-morrow we would sit i' the consistory,
    And there determine of his punishment?
    You brought us word even now, it was decreed
    That Bruno and the cursed Emperor
    Were by the holy council both condemn'd
    For loathed Lollards and base schismatics:
    Then wherefore would you have me view that book?
CARDINAL OF FRANCE. Your grace mistakes; you gave us no such
    charge.
RAYMOND. Deny it not; we all are witnesses
    That Bruno here was late deliver'd you,
    With his rich triple crown to be reserv'd
    And put into the church's treasury.
BOTH CARDINALS. By holy Paul, we saw them not!
POPE. By Peter, you shall die,
    Unless you bring them forth immediately!—
    Hale them to[218] prison, lade their limbs with gyves.—
    False prelates, for this hateful treachery
    Curs'd be your souls to hellish misery!

[*Exeunt* ATTENDANTS *with the two* CARDINALS.]

FAUSTUS. So, they are safe. Now, Faustus, to the feast:
    The Pope had never such a frolic guest.
POPE. Lord Archbishop of Rheims, sit down with us.
ARCHBISHOP.[219] I thank your Holiness.
FAUSTUS. Fall to; the devil choke you,[220] an you spare!
POPE. Who is that spoke?—Friars, look about.—
    Lord Raymond, pray, fall to. I am beholding[221]
    To the Bishop of Milan for this so rare a present.

---

[217] *Be*: So 4tos 1616, 1624.—2to 1631 "are."

[218] *Them to*: So 4to 1616.—2tos 1624, 1631, "them *forth* to."

[219] *Archbishop*.: Old eds. "Bish." and "Bishop" (and so afterwards).

[220] *You*: So 4tos 1616, 1631.—Not in 4to 1624.

[221] *Beholding*: So 4to 1616 (see note).—2tos 1624, 1631, "beholden."

Note from (Doctor Faustus, from the quarto of 1604):

"Beholding: i.e. beholden."

FAUSTUS. I thank you, sir. [*Snatches the dish.*]

POPE. How now! who snatch'd the meat from me?
Villains, why speak you not?—
My good Lord Archbishop, here's a most dainty dish
Was sent me from a cardinal in France.

FAUSTUS. I'll have that too. [*Snatches the dish.*]

POPE. What Lollards do attend our holiness,
That we receive such[222] great indignity?
Fetch me some wine.

FAUSTUS. Ay, pray, do, for Faustus is a-dry.

POPE. Lord Raymond,
I drink unto your grace.

FAUSTUS. I pledge your grace. [*Snatches the cup.*]

POPE. My wine gone too!—Ye lubbers, look about,
And find the man that doth this villany,
Or, by our sanctitude, you all shall die!—
I pray, my lords, have patience at this
Troublesome banquet.

ARCHBISHOP. Please it[223] your Holiness, I think it be some ghost crept out of Purgatory, and now is come unto your Holiness for his pardon.

POPE. It may be so.—
Go, then, command our priests to sing a dirge,
To lay the fury of this same troublesome ghost.

[*Exit an* ATTENDANT.—*The* POPE *crosses himself.*]

FAUSTUS. How now! must every bit be spic'd with a cross?—
Nay, then, take that. [*Strikes the* POPE.]

POPE. O, I am slain!—Help me, my lords!
O, come and help to bear my body hence!—
Damn'd be his[224] soul for ever for this deed!

[*Exeunt all except* FAUSTUS *and* MEPHISTOPHILIS.]

MEPHISTOPHILIS. Now, Faustus, what will you do now? for I can tell you you'll be cursed with bell, book, and candle.

FAUSTUS. Bell, book, and candle,—candle, book, and bell,—
Forward and backward, to curse Faustus to hell!

[*Re-enter the* FRIARS, *with bell, book, and candle, for the Dirge.*]

---

[222] Such: So 4tos 1616, 1631.—2to 1624 "this."
[223] It: So 4to 1616.—Not in 4tos 1624, 1631.
[224] *His*: So 4tos 1624, 1631.—2to 1616 "this."

FIRST FRIAR. Come, brethren, lets about our business with good devotion. [*They sing.*]

> *Cursed be he that stole his Holiness' meat from the table!*
> maledicat Dominus!
> *Cursed be he that struck*[225] *his Holiness a blow on*[226] *the face!*
> maledicat Dominus!
> *Cursed be he that struck Friar Sandelo a blow on the pate!*
> maledicat Dominus!
> *Cursed be he that disturbeth our holy dirge!* maledicat Dominus!
> *Cursed be he that took away his Holiness' wine!* maledicat
> Dominus!

[MEPHISTOPHILIS *and* FAUSTUS *beat the* FRIARS, *and fling fireworks among them, and exeunt.*]

[*Enter* ROBIN *and* DICK *with a cup.*]

DICK. Sirrah Robin, we were best look that your devil can answer the stealing of this same[227] cup, for the Vintner's boy follows us at the hard heels.[228]

ROBIN. 'Tis no matter; let him come: an he follow us, I'll so conjure him as he was never conjured in his life, I warrant him.
Let me see the cup.

DICK. Here 'tis. [*Gives the cup to* ROBIN.]
Yonder he comes: now, Robin, now or never shew thy cunning.

[*Enter* VINTNER.[229]]

VINTNER. O, are you here? I am glad I have found you. You are a couple of fine companions: pray, where's the cup you stole from the tavern?

---

[225] *Struck*: Here the old eds. have "stroke" and "strooke:" but in the next clause they all agree in having "strucke."

[226] *On*: So 4tos 1624, 1631.—Not in 4to 1616.

[227] *Same*: So 4tos 1616, 1624.—Not in 4to 1631.

[228] *At the hard heels*: The modern editors, ignorant of the old phraseology, thought that they corrected this passage in printing "hard at the heels."

[229] *Vintner*: So all the old eds.; and presently Robin addresses this person as "vintner:" yet Dick has just spoken of him as "the Vintner's boy." See note.

Note from (Doctor Faustus, from the quarto of 1604):

"*Drawer*: There is an inconsistency here: the Vintner cannot properly be addressed as "Drawer." The later 4tos are also inconsistent in the corresponding passage: Dick says, "*the vintner's boy* follows us at the hard heels," and immediately the "*vintner*" enters."

ROBIN. How, how! we steal a cup! take heed what you say: we look not
　　like cup-stealers, I can tell you.
VINTNER. Never deny't, for I know you have it; and I'll search you.
ROBIN. Search me! ay, and spare not.
　　—Hold the cup, Dick [Aside to DICK, giving him the cup].—
　　Come, come, search me, search me.

　　　　[VINTNER *searches him*.]

VINTNER. Come on, sirrah, let me search you now.
DICK. Ay, ay, do, do.
　　—Hold the cup, Robin [Aside to ROBIN, giving him the cup].—
　　I fear not your searching: we scorn to steal your[230] cups,
　　I can tell you.

　　　　[VINTNER *searches him*.]

VINTNER. Never out-face me for the matter; for, sure, the cup is
　　between you two.
ROBIN. Nay, there you lie; 'tis beyond us both.
VINTNER. A plague take you! I thought 'twas your knavery to take it
　　away: come, give it me again.
ROBIN. Ay, much![231] when, can you tell?—Dick, make me a circle, and
　　stand close at my back, and stir not for thy life.—Vintner, you
　　shall have your cup anon.—Say nothing, Dick.—[*Reads from a
　　book*] O per se, O; Demogorgon; Belcher, and Mephistophilis!

　　　　[*Enter* MEPHISTOPHILIS.]

MEPHISTOPHILIS. You princely legions of infernal rule,
　　How am I vexed by these villains' charms!
　　From Constantinople have they brought me now,
　　Only for pleasure of these damned slaves.

　　　　[*Exit* VINTNER.]

ROBIN. By lady,[232] sir, you have had a shrewd journey of it! will it
　　please you to[233] take a shoulder of mutton to supper, and a tester[234]
　　in your purse, and go back again?

---

　　　[230] *Your*: So 4tos 1616, 1631.—Not in 4to 1624.
　　　[231] *Much*: Equivalent to—by no means, not at all. This ironical exclamation is very
common in our old dramatists. (Mr. Hunter,—*New Illust. of Shakespeare*, ii. 56,—
explains it very differently.)
　　　[232] *By lady*: i.e. By our Lady.
　　　[233] *To*: So 4tos 1616, 1624.—Not in 4to 1631.

DICK. Ay, I pray you heartily, sir; for we called you but in jest,
I promise you.

MEPHISTOPHILIS. To purge the rashness of this cursed deed,
First, be thou turned to this ugly shape,
For apish deeds transformed to an ape.

ROBIN. O, brave! an ape! I pray, sir, let me have the carrying of him
about, to shew some tricks.

MEPHISTOPHILIS. And so thou shalt: be thou transformed to a dog, and
carry him upon thy back. Away! be gone!

ROBIN. A dog! that's excellent: let the maids look well to their
porridge-pots, for I'll into the kitchen presently.—Come, Dick,
come.

[*Exeunt* ROBIN *and* DICK.]

MEPHISTOPHILIS. Now with the flames of ever-burning fire
I'll wing myself, and forthwith fly amain
Unto my Faustus, to the Great Turk's court. [*Exit.*]

[*Enter* MARTINO *and* FREDERICK *at several doors.*]

MARTINO. What, ho, officers, gentlemen!
Hie to the presence to attend the Emperor.—
Good Frederick, see the rooms be voided straight:
His majesty is coming to the hall;
Go back, and see the state[235] in readiness.

FREDERICK. But where is Bruno, our elected Pope,
That on a Fury's back came post from Rome?
Will not his grace consort the Emperor?

MARTINO. O, yes; and with him comes the German conjurer,
The learned Faustus, fame of Wittenberg,
The wonder of the world for magic art;
And he intends to shew great Carolus
The race of all his stout progenitors,
And bring in presence of his majesty
The royal shapes and perfect[236] semblances
Of Alexander and his beauteous paramour.

FREDERICK. Where is Benvolio?

MARTINO. Fast asleep, I warrant you;
He took his rouse[237] with stoops of Rhenish wine
So kindly yesternight to Bruno's health,

---

[234] *Tester*: i.e. sixpence.

[235] *The state*: i.e. the raised chair or throne, with a canopy.

[236] *Perfect*: So 4tos 1624, 1631.—2to 1616 "warlike."

[237] *Rouse*: i.e. bumper.

That all this day the sluggard keeps his bed.
FREDERICK. See, see, his window's ope! we'll call to him.
MARTINO. What, ho! Benvolio!

[*Enter* BENVOLIO *above, at a window, in his nightcap, buttoning.*]

BENVOLIO. What a devil ail you two?
MARTINO. Speak softly, sir, lest the devil hear you;
    For Faustus at the court is late arriv'd,
    And at his heels a[238] thousand Furies wait,
    To accomplish whatsoe'er the doctor please.
BENVOLIO. What of this?
MARTINO. Come, leave thy chamber first, and thou shalt see
    This conjurer perform such rare exploits,
    Before the Pope and royal Emperor,
    As never yet was seen in Germany.
BENVOLIO. Has not the Pope enough of conjuring yet?
    He was upon the devil's back late enough:
    An if he be so far in love with him,
    I would he would post with him to Rome again!
FREDERICK. Speak, wilt thou come and see this sport?
BENVOLIO. Not I.
MARTINO. Wilt thou stand in thy window, and see it, then?
BENVOLIO. Ay, an I fall not asleep i' the mean time.
MARTINO. The Emperor is at hand, who comes to see
    What wonders by black spells may compass'd be.
BENVOLIO. Well, go you attend the Emperor. I am content, for this
    once, to thrust my head out at a[239] window; for they say, if a man
    be drunk over night, the devil cannot hurt him in the morning: if
    that be true, I have a charm in my head, shall control him as well
    as the conjurer, I warrant you.

[*Exeunt* FREDERICK *and* MARTINO.]

[*A Sennet. Enter* CHARLES *the German Emperor,* BRUNO, *Duke of*
    SAXONY, FAUSTUS, MEPHISTOPHILIS, FREDERICK, MARTINO,
    and Attendants.]

---

[238] *A*: So 4to 1616.—2tos 1624, 1631, "ten."
[239] *A*: So 4tos 1616, 1624.—2to 1631 "the."

EMPEROR. Wonder of men, renowm'd[240] magician,
Thrice-learned Faustus, welcome to our court.
This deed of thine, in setting Bruno free
From his and our professed enemy,
Shall add more excellence unto thine art
Than if by powerful necromantic spells
Thou couldst command the world's obedience:
For ever be belov'd of Carolus!
And if this Bruno, thou hast late redeem'd,
In peace possess the triple diadem,
And sit in Peter's chair, despite of chance,
Thou shalt be famous through[241] all Italy,
And honour'd of the German Emperor.
FAUSTUS. These[242] gracious words, most royal Carolus,
Shall make poor Faustus, to his utmost power,
Both love and serve the German Emperor,
And lay his life at holy Bruno's feet:
For proof whereof, if so your grace be pleas'd,
The doctor stands prepar'd by power of art
To cast his magic charms, that shall pierce through[243]
The ebon gates of ever-burning hell,
And hale the stubborn Furies from their caves,
To compass whatsoe'er your grace commands.
BENVOLIO. Blood, he speaks terribly! but, for all that, I do not greatly
believe him: he looks as like a[244] conjurer as the Pope to a
costermonger. [*Aside.*]
EMPEROR. Then, Faustus, as thou late didst promise us,
We would behold that famous conqueror,
Great Alexander, and his paramour,
In their true shapes and state majestical,
That we may wonder at their excellence.
FAUSTUS. Your majesty shall see them presently.—

---

[240] *Renowm'd*: Old eds. "renown'd"; but earlier, p. 109, first col., 4to 1616 has "renowm'd": see note 23 and see note.

Note from p. 11. (The First Part of Tamburlaine the Great):

"*Renowmed*: i.e. renowned.—So the 8vo.—The 4to "renowned."—The form "*renowmed*" (Fr. *renomme*) occurs repeatedly afterwards in this play, according to the 8vo. It is occasionally found in writers posterior to Marlowe's time. e.g.
"Of Constantines great towne *renowm'd* in vaine."
Verses to King James, prefixed to Lord Stirling's
Monarchicke Tragedies, ed. 1607."

[241] *Through*: So 4tos 1616, 1624.—2to 1631 "thorow."
[242] *These*: So 4to 1616.—2tos 1624, 1631, "Those."
[243] *Through*: So 4tos 1616, 1624.—2to 1631 "thorow."
[244] *A*: So 4tos 1624, 1631.—Not in 4to 1616.

Mephistophilis, away,
And, with a solemn noise of trumpets' sound,
Present before this[245] royal Emperor
Great Alexander and his beauteous paramour.

MEPHISTOPHILIS. Faustus, I will. [*Exit.*]

BENVOLIO. Well, Master Doctor, an your devils come not away quickly, you shall have me asleep presently: zounds, I could eat myself for anger, to think I have been such an ass all this while, to stand gaping after the devil's governor, and can see nothing!

FAUSTUS. I'll make you feel something anon, if my art fail me not.—
My lord, I must forewarn your majesty,
That, when my spirits present the royal shapes
Of Alexander and his paramour,
Your grace demand[246] no questions of the king,
But in dumb silence let them come and go.

EMPEROR. Be it as Faustus please; we are content.

BENVOLIO. Ay, ay, and I am content too: an thou bring Alexander and his paramour before the Emperor, I'll be Actæon, and turn myself to a stag.

FAUSTUS. And I'll play Diana, and send you the horns presently.

[*Sennet. Enter, at one door,[247] the* EMPEROR ALEXANDER, *at the other,* DARIUS. *They meet.* DARIUS *is thrown down*; ALEXANDER *kills him, takes off his crown, and, offering to go out, his* PARAMOUR *meets him. He embraceth her, and sets* DARIUS' *crown upon her head; and, coming back, both salute the* EMPEROR, *who, leaving his state,[248] offers to embrace them; which* FAUSTUS *seeing, suddenly stays him. Then trumpets cease, and music sounds.*]

My gracious lord, you do forget yourself;
These[249] are but shadows, not substantial.

EMPEROR. O, pardon me! my thoughts are so ravish'd
With sight of this renowmed[250] emperor,
That in mine arms I would have compass'd him.
But, Faustus, since I may not speak to them,
To satisfy my longing thoughts[251] at full,
Let me this tell thee: I have heard it said

---

[245] *This*: So 4to 1616.—2tos 1624, 1631, "the."
[246] *Demand*: So 4tos 1616, 1631.—2to 1624 "demands."
[247] *Door*: So 4tos 1624, 1631.—Not in 4to 1616.
[248] *State*: See note 235, p. 37. i.e.—So 4tos 1616, 1631.—2to 1624 "seat."
[249] *These*: So 4to 1616.—2tos 1624, 1631, "They."
[250] *Renowmed*: Old eds. "renowned." See note 240, p. 39. i.e.
[251] *Thoughts*: So 4tos 1616, 1631.—2to 1624 "thought."

That this fair lady, whilst[252] she liv'd on earth,
Had on her neck a little wart or mole;
How may I prove that saying to be true?
FAUSTUS. Your majesty may boldly go and see.
EMPEROR. Faustus, I see it plain;
And in this sight thou better pleasest me
Than if I gain'd[253] another monarchy.
FAUSTUS. Away! be gone! [*Exit show.*]—See, see, my gracious lord!
what strange beast is yon, that thrusts his head out at window?[254]
EMPEROR. O, wondrous sight!—See, Duke of Saxony,
Two spreading horns most strangely fastened
Upon the head of young Benvolio!
SAXONY. What, is he asleep or dead?
FAUSTUS. He sleeps, my lord; but dreams not of his horns.
EMPEROR. This sport is excellent: we'll call and wake him.—
What, ho, Benvolio!
BENVOLIO. A plague upon you! let me sleep a while.
EMPEROR. I blame thee not to sleep much, having such a head of thine
own.
SAXONY. Look up, Benvolio; 'tis the Emperor calls.
BENVOLIO. The Emperor! where?—O, zounds, my head!
EMPEROR. Nay, an thy horns hold, 'tis no matter for thy head, for that's
armed sufficiently.
FAUSTUS. Why, how now, Sir Knight! what, hanged by the horns! this
is[255] most horrible: fie, fie, pull in your head, for shame! let not all
the world wonder at you.
BENVOLIO. Zounds, doctor, this is[256] your villany!
FAUSTUS. O, say not so, sir! the doctor has no skill,
No art, no cunning, to present these lords,
Or bring before this royal Emperor
The mighty monarch, warlike Alexander.
If Faustus do it, you are straight resolv'd,
In bold Actæon's shape, to turn a stag:—
And therefore, my lord, so please your majesty,
I'll raise a kennel of hounds shall hunt him so
As[257] all his footmanship shall scarce prevail
To keep his carcass from their bloody fangs.—
Ho, Belimoth, Argiron, Asteroth![258]

---

[252] *Whilst*: So 4to 1616.—2tos 1624, 1631, "while."
[253] *I gain'd*: So 4tos 1616, 1631.—2to 1624 "I *had* gain'd."
[254] *At window*: So 4to 1616.—2tos 1624, 1631, "at *the* window."
[255] *Is*: So 4tos 1624, 1631.—Not in 4to 1616.
[256] *This is*: So 4to 1624 (and rightly, as the next line proves).—2tos 1616, 1631, "is this."
[257] *As*: So 4to 1616.—2to 1624 "That."—2to 1631 "And."
[258] *Belimoth....Asteroth*: Old eds. here "Belimote (and "Belimot") Asterote": but see p. 45.

BENVOLIO. Hold, hold!—Zounds, he'll raise up a kennel of devils, I
   think, anon.—Good my lord, entreat for me.—'Sblood, I am never
   able to endure these torments.

EMPEROR. Then, good Master Doctor,
   Let me entreat you to remove his horns;
   He has[259] done penance now sufficiently.

FAUSTUS. My gracious lord, not so much for injury done to me, as to
   delight your majesty with some mirth, hath Faustus justly requited
   this injurious knight; which being all I desire, I am content to
   remove   his   horns.[260]—Mephistophilis,   transform   him
   [MEPHISTOPHILIS *removes the horns*]:—and hereafter, sir,[261] look
   you speak well of scholars.

BENVOLIO. Speak well of ye! 'sblood, an scholars be such cuckold-
   makers, to clap horns of[262] honest men's heads o' this order, I'll
   ne'er trust smooth faces and small ruffs more.—But, an I be not
   revenged for this, would I might be turned to a gaping oyster, and
   drink nothing but salt water! [*Aside, and then exit above.*]

EMPEROR. Come, Faustus: while the Emperor lives,
   In recompense of this thy high desert,
   Thou shalt command the state of Germany,
   And live belov'd of mighty Carolus. [*Exeunt.*]

[*Enter* BENVOLIO, MARTINO, FREDERICK, *and* SOLDIERS.]

MARTINO. Nay, sweet Benvolio, let us sway[263] thy thoughts
   From this attempt against the conjurer.[264]

---

[259] *Has*: So 4to 1616.—2tos 1624, 1631, "hath."
[260] *Horns*: So 4tos 1616, 1631.—2to 1624 "horne."
[261] *Sir*: So 4tos 1616, 1631.—Not in 4to 1624.
[262] *Of*: i.e. on.
[263] *Sway*: So 4tos 1616, 1631.—2to 1624 "stay."
[264] *This attempt against the conjurer*: See note.

Note from (Doctor Faustus, from the quarto of 1604):

"Mephistophilis, transform him straight: According to THE HISTORY OF DR.
FAUSTUS, the knight was not present during Faustus's "conference" with the Emperor;
nor did he offer the doctor any insult by doubting his skill in magic. We are there told
that Faustus happening to see the knight asleep, "leaning out of a window of the great
hall," fixed a huge pair of hart's horns on his head; "and, as the knight awaked, thinking
to pull in his head, he hit his hornes against the glasse, that the panes thereof flew about
his eares: thinke here how this good gentleman was vexed, for he could neither get
backward nor forward." After the emperor and the courtiers, to their great amusement,
had beheld the poor knight in this condition, Faustus removed the horns. When Faustus,
having taken leave of the emperor, was a league and a half from the city, he was attacked
in a wood by the knight and some of his companions: they were in armour, and mounted
on fair palfreys; but the doctor quickly overcame them by turning all the bushes into
horsemen, and "so charmed them, that every one, knight and other, for the space of a

BENVOLIO. Away! you love me not, to urge me thus:
    Shall I let slip so great an injury,
    When every servile groom jests at my wrongs,
    And in their rustic gambols proudly say,
    "Benvolio's head was grac'd with horns today?"
    O, may these eyelids never close again,
    Till with my sword I have that[265] conjurer slain!
    If you will aid me in this enterprise,
    Then draw your weapons and be resolute;
    If not, depart: here will Benvolio die,
    But Faustus' death shall quit my[266] infamy.
FREDERICK. Nay, we will stay with thee, betide what may,
    And kill that[267] doctor, if he come this way.
BENVOLIO. Then, gentle Frederick, hie thee to the grove,
    And place our servants and our followers
    Close in an[268] ambush there behind the trees.
    By this, I know the conjurer is near:
    I saw him kneel, and kiss the Emperor's hand,
    And take his leave, laden with rich rewards.
    Then, soldiers, boldly[269] fight: if Faustus die,
    Take you the wealth, leave us the victory.
FREDERICK. Come, soldiers, follow me unto the grove:
    Who kills him shall have gold and endless love.

[*Exit* FREDERICK *with* SOLDIERS.]

BENVOLIO. My head is lighter, than it was, by the horns;
    But yet my heart's[270] more ponderous than my head,
    And pants until I see that[271] conjurer dead.
MARTINO. Where shall we place ourselves, Benvolio?
BENVOLIO. Here will we stay to bide the first assault:
    O, were that damned hell-hound but in place,
    Thou soon shouldst see me quit my foul disgrace!

---

whole moneth, did weare a paire of goates hornes on their browes, and every palfry a paire of oxe hornes on his head; and this was their penance appointed by Faustus." A second attempt of the knight to revenge himself on Faustus proved equally unsuccessful. Sigs. G 2, I 3, ed. 1648."

[265] *That*: So 4to 1616.—2tos 1624, 1631, "the."
[266] *My*: So 4to 1616.—2tos 1624, 1631, "thy."
[267] *That*: So 4to 1616.—2tos 1624, 1631, "the."
[268] *An*: So 4to 1616.—Not in 4tos 1624, 1631.
[269] *Boldly*: So 4to 1616.—2tos 1624, 1631, "brauely."
[270] *Heart's*: So 4tos 1624, 1631.—2to 1616 "heart."
[271] *That*: So 4to 1616.—2tos 1624, 1631, "the."

[*Re-enter* FREDERICK.]

FREDERICK. Close, close! the conjurer is at hand,
  And all alone comes walking in his gown;
  Be ready, then, and strike the[272] peasant down.
BENVOLIO. Mine be that honour, then. Now, sword, strike home!
  For horns he gave I'll have his head anon.
MARTINO. See, see, he comes!

[*Enter* FAUSTUS *with a false head.*]

BENVOLIO. No words. This blow ends all:
  Hell take his soul! his body thus must fall.

[*Stabs* FAUSTUS.]

FAUSTUS. [*Falling.*] O!
FREDERICK. Groan you, Master Doctor?
BENVOLIO. Break may his heart with groans!—Dear Frederick, see,
  Thus will I end his griefs immediately.
MARTINO. Strike with a willing hand.

[BENVOLIO *strikes off* FAUSTUS' *head.*]

  His head is off.
BENVOLIO. The devil's dead; the Furies now[273] may laugh.
FREDERICK. Was this that stern aspect, that awful frown,
  Made the grim monarch of infernal spirits
  Tremble and quake at his commanding charms?
MARTINO. Was this that damned head, whose art[274] conspir'd
  Benvolio's shame before the Emperor?
BENVOLIO. Ay, that's the head, and there[275] the body lies,
  Justly rewarded for his villanies.
FREDERICK. Come, let's devise how we may add more shame
  To the black scandal of his hated name.
BENVOLIO. First, on his head, in quittance of my wrongs,
  I'll nail huge forked horns, and let them hang
  Within the window where he yok'd me first,
  That all the world may see my just revenge.
MARTINO. What use shall we put his beard to?

---

[272] *The*: So 4to 1616.—2tos 1624, 1631, "that."
[273] *Now*: so 4to 1616.—Not in 4tos 1624, 1631.
[274] *Art*: Old eds. "heart" (which, after all, may be right).
[275] *There*: So 4tos 1624, 1631.—2to 1616 "here."

BENVOLIO. We'll sell it to a chimney-sweeper: it will wear out ten
 birchen brooms, I warrant you.
FREDERICK. What shall his[276] eyes do?
BENVOLIO. We'll pull[277] out his eyes; and they shall serve for buttons
 to his lips, to keep his tongue from catching cold.
MARTINO. An excellent policy! and now, sirs, having divided him,
 what shall the body do? [FAUSTUS *rises.*]
BENVOLIO. Zounds, the devil's alive again!
FREDERICK. Give him his head, for God's sake.
FAUSTUS. Nay, keep it: Faustus will have heads and hands,
 Ay, all[278] your hearts to recompense this deed.
 Knew you not, traitors, I was limited
 For four-and-twenty years to breathe on earth?
 And, had you cut my body with your swords,
 Or hew'd this flesh and bones as small as sand,
 Yet in a minute had my spirit return'd,
 And I had breath'd a man, made free from harm.
 But wherefore do I dally my revenge?—
 Asteroth, Belimoth, Mephistophilis?

 [*Enter* MEPHISTOPHILIS, *and other* DEVILS.]

 Go, horse these traitors on your fiery backs,
 And mount aloft with them as high as heaven:
 Thence pitch them headlong to the lowest hell.
 Yet, stay: the world shall see their misery,
 And hell shall after plague their treachery.
 Go, Belimoth, and take this caitiff hence,
 And hurl him in some lake of mud and dirt.
 Take thou this other, drag him through[279] the woods
 Amongst[280] the pricking thorns and sharpest briers;
 Whilst, with my gentle Mephistophilis,
 This traitor flies unto some steepy rock,
 That, rolling down, may break the villain's bones,
 As he intended to dismember me.
 Fly hence; despatch my charge immediately.
FREDERICK. Pity us, gentle Faustus! save our lives!
FAUSTUS. Away!
FREDERICK. He must needs go that the devil drives.

---

[276] *His*: So 4tos 1624, 1631.—Not in 3to sic 1616.
[277] *Pull*: So 4tos 1624, 1631.—2to 1616 "put."
[278] *All*: Old eds. "call."
[279] *Through*: So 4tos 1616, 1624.—2to 1631 "thorow."
[280] *Amongst*: So 4to 1616.—2tos 1624, 1631, "Among."

[*Exeunt* MEPHISTOPHILIS *and* DEVILS *with* BENVOLIO, MARTINO,
    and FREDERICK.]

[*Enter the ambushed* SOLDIERS.[281]]

FIRST SOLDIER. Come, sirs, prepare yourselves in readiness;
    Make haste to help these noble gentlemen:
    I heard them parley with the conjurer.
SECOND SOLDIER. See, where he comes! despatch and kill the slave.
FAUSTUS. What's here? an ambush to betray my life!
    Then, Faustus, try thy skill.—Base peasants, stand!
    For, lo, these[282] trees remove at my command,
    And stand as bulwarks 'twixt yourselves and me,
    To shield me from your hated treachery!
    Yet, to encounter this your weak attempt,
    Behold, an army comes incontinent!

[FAUSTUS *strikes the door,*[283] *and enter a* DEVIL *playing on a
    drum; after him another, bearing an ensign; and divers with
    weapons;* MEPHISTOPHILIS *with fire-works. They set upon the*
    SOLDIERS, *drive them out, and exeunt.*]

[*Enter, at several doors,* BENVOLIO, FREDERICK, *and* MARTINO,
    *their heads and faces bloody, and besmeared with mud and
    dirt; all having horns on their heads.*]

MARTINO. What, ho, Benvolio!
BENVOLIO. Here.—What, Frederick, ho!
FREDERICK. O, help me, gentle friend!—Where is Martino?
MARTINO. Dear Frederick, here,
    Half smother'd in a lake of mud and dirt,
    Through which the Furies dragg'd me by the heels.
FREDERICK. Martino, see, Benvolio's horns again!
MARTINO. O, misery!—How now, Benvolio!
BENVOLIO. Defend me, heaven! shall I be haunted still?
MARTINO. Nay, fear not, man; we have no power to kill.
BENVOLIO. My friends transformed thus! O, hellish spite!
    Your heads are all set with horns.
FREDERICK. You hit it right;
    It is your own you mean; feel on your head.

---

[281] *Enter the ambushed Soldiers*: Here (though it seems that Faustus does not quit
the stage) a change of scene is supposed.
    [282] *These*: So 4to 1616.—2tos 1624, 1631, "the."
    [283] *The door*: i.e. the stage-door,—the writer here addressing himself to *the actor*
only, for the scene lies in a wood.

BENVOLIO. Zounds,[284] horns again!

MARTINO. Nay, chafe not, man; we all are[285] sped.

BENVOLIO. What devil attends this damn'd magician,
That, spite of spite, our wrongs are doubled?

FREDERICK. What may we do, that we may hide our shames?

BENVOLIO. If we should follow him to work revenge,
He'd join long asses' ears to these huge horns,
And make us laughing-stocks to all the world.

MARTINO. What shall we, then, do, dear Benvolio?

BENVOLIO. I have a castle joining near these woods;
And thither we'll repair, and live obscure,
Till time shall alter these[286] our brutish shapes:
Sith black disgrace hath thus eclips'd our fame,
We'll rather die with grief than live with shame. [*Exeunt.*]

[*Enter* FAUSTUS, *a* HORSE-COURSER, *and* MEPHISTOPHILIS.]

HORSE-COURSER. I beseech your worship, accept of these forty dollars.

FAUSTUS. Friend, thou canst not buy so good a horse for so small a price. I have no great need to sell him: but, if thou likest him for ten dollars more, take him, because I see thou hast a good mind to him.

HORSE-COURSER. I beseech you, sir, accept of this: I am a very poor man, and have lost very much of late by horse-flesh, and this bargain will set me up again.

FAUSTUS. Well, I will not stand with thee: give me the money [HORSE-COURSER *gives* FAUSTUS *the money*]. Now, sirrah, I must tell you that you may ride him o'er hedge and ditch, and spare him not; but, do you hear? in any case, ride him not into the water.

HORSE-COURSER. How, sir! not into the water! why, will he not drink of all waters?

FAUSTUS. Yes, he will drink of all waters; but ride him not into the water: o'er hedge and ditch, or where thou wilt, but not into the water. Go, bid the hostler deliver him unto you, and remember what I say.

HORSE-COURSER. I warrant you, sir!—O, joyful day! now am I a made man for ever. [*Exit.*]

FAUSTUS. What art thou, Faustus, but a man condemn'd to die?
Thy fatal time draws to a final end;
Despair doth drive distrust into my thoughts:
Confound these passions with a quiet sleep:

---

[284] *Zounds*: So 4tos 1624, 1631.—2to 1616, "Zons."

[285] *All are*: So 4to 1616.—2tos 1624, 1631, "are all."

[286] *These*: So 4tos 1624, 1631.—2to 1616 "this."

Tush, Christ did call the thief upon the Cross;
Then rest thee, Faustus, quiet in conceit. [*He sits to sleep.*]

[*Re-enter the* HORSE-COURSER, *wet.*]

HORSE-COURSER. 0, what a cozening doctor was this! I, riding my
horse into the water, thinking some hidden mystery had been in the
horse, I had nothing under me but a little straw, and had much ado
to escape[287] drowning. Well, I'll go rouse him, and make him give
me my forty dollars again.—Ho, sirrah Doctor, you cozening scab!
Master Doctor, awake, and rise, and give me my money again, for
your horse is turned to a bottle of hay, Master Doctor! [*He pulls off*
FAUSTUS' *leg*]. Alas, I am undone! What shall I do? I have pulled
off his leg.
FAUSTUS. O, help, help! the villain hath murdered me.
HORSE-COURSER. Murder or not murder, now he has[288] but one leg, I'll
outrun him, and cast this leg into some ditch or other. [*Aside, and
then runs out.*]
FAUSTUS. Stop him, stop him, stop him!—Ha, ha, ha! Faustus hath his
leg again, and the Horse-courser a bundle of hay for his forty
dollars.

[*Enter* WAGNER.]

How now, Wagner! what news with thee?
WAGNER. If it please you, the Duke of Vanholt doth earnestly entreat
your company, and hath sent some of his men to attend you,[289]
with provision fit for your journey.
FAUSTUS. The Duke of Vanholt's an honourable gentleman, and one to
whom I must be no niggard of my cunning. Come, away! [*Exeunt.*]

[*Enter* ROBIN, DICK, *the* HORSE-COURSER, *and a* CARTER.]

CARTER. Come, my masters, I'll bring you to the best beer in
Europe.—What, ho, hostess! where be these whores?

[*Enter* HOSTESS.]

HOSTESS. How now! what lack you? What, my old guess![290] welcome.
ROBIN. Sirrah Dick, dost thou[291] know why I stand so mute?

---

[287] *Escape*: So 4tos 1616, 1631.—2to 1624 "scape."
[288] *Has*: So 4tos 1616, 1624.—2to 1631 "hath."
[289] *You*: So 4to 1616.—Not in 4tos 1624, 1631.
[290] *Guess*: A corruption of guests (very frequent in our early dramatists) which
occurs again at p. 130. first col. So 4to 1616.—2tos 1624, 1631, "guests." See note 315.

DICK. No, Robin: why is't?

ROBIN. I am eighteen-pence on the score. but say nothing; see if she have forgotten me.

HOSTESS. Who's this that stands so solemnly by himself? What, my old guest!

ROBIN. O, hostess, how do you? I hope my score stands still.

HOSTESS. Ay, there's no doubt of that; for methinks you make no haste to wipe it out.

DICK. Why, hostess, I say, fetch us some beer.

HOSTESS. You shall presently.—Look up into the hall there, ho!

[*Exit.—Drink is presently brought in.*]

DICK. Come, sirs, what shall we do now[292] till mine hostess comes?

CARTER. Marry, sir,[293] I'll tell you the bravest tale how a conjurer served me. You know Doctor Faustus?

HORSE-COURSER. Ay, a plague take him! here's some on's have cause to know him. Did he conjure thee too?

CARTER. I'll tell you how he served me. As I was going to Wittenberg, t'other day,[294] with a load of hay, he met me, and asked me what he should give me for as much hay as he could eat. Now, sir, I thinking that a little would serve his turn, bad him take as much as he would for three farthings: so he presently gave me my[295] money and fell to eating; and, as I am a cursen[296] man, he never left eating till he had eat up all my load of hay.

ALL. O, monstrous! eat a whole load of hay!

ROBIN. Yes, yes, that may be; for I have heard of one that has eat a load of logs.

HORSE-COURSER. Now, sirs, you shall hear how villanously he served me. I went to him yesterday to buy a horse of him, and he would by no means sell him under forty dollars. So, sir, because I knew him to be such a horse as would run over hedge and ditch and never tire, I gave him his money. So, when I had my horse, Doctor Faustus bad me ride him night and day, and spare him no time; but, quoth he, in any case, ride him not into the water. Now, sir, I thinking the horse had had some quality[297] that he would not have

---

[291] *Thou*: So 4to 1616.—Not in 4tos 1624, 1631.

[292] *Now*: So 4to 1616.—Not in 4tos 1624, 1631.

[293] *Sir*: Qy. "sirs"? but see the next speech of the Carter, and the next speech but one of the Horse-courser, who, in his narrative, uses both "sirs" and "sir."

[294] *As I was going to Wittenberg, t'other day, &c.*: See *The History of Doctor Faustus*, Chap. xxxv,—"How Doctor Faustus eat a load of hay."—The Carter does not appear in the earlier play.

[295] *My*: So 4to 1616.—Not in 4tos 1624, 1631.

[296] *Cursen*: i.e. christened.

[297] *Some quality*: So 4to 1616.—2tos 1624, 1631, "some *rare* quality."

me know of, what did I but rid[298] him into a great river? and when
I came just in the midst, my horse vanished away, and I sate
straddling upon a bottle of hay.

ALL. O, brave doctor!

HORSE-COURSER. But you shall hear how bravely I served him for it. I
went me home to his house, and there I found him asleep. I kept a
hallooing and whooping in his ears; but all could not wake him. I,
seeing that, took him by the leg, and never rested pulling till I had
pulled me his leg quite off; and now 'tis at home in mine hostry.

ROBIN. And has the doctor but one leg, then? that's excellent; for one
of his devils turned me into the likeness of an ape's face.

CARTER. Some more drink, hostess!

ROBIN. Hark you, we'll into another room and drink a while, and then
we'll go seek out the doctor. [*Exeunt.*]

[*Enter the* DUKE OF VANHOLT, *his* DUCHESS, FAUSTUS,
MEPHISTOPHILIS, *and* ATTENDANTS.]

DUKE. Thanks, Master Doctor, for these pleasant sights; nor know I
how sufficiently to recompense your great deserts in erecting that
enchanted castle in the air,[299] the sight whereof so delighted[300] me
as nothing in the world could please me more.

FAUSTUS. I do think myself, my good lord, highly recompensed in that
it pleaseth[301] your grace to think but well of that which Faustus
hath performed.—But, gracious lady, it may be that you have taken
no pleasure in those sights; therefore, I pray you tell me, what is
the thing you most desire to have; be it in the world, it shall be
yours: I have heard that great-bellied women do long for things are
rare and dainty.

DUCHESS. True, Master Doctor; and, since I find you so kind, I will
make known unto you what my heart desires to have; and, were it
now summer, as it is January, a dead time of the winter, I would
request no better meat than a dish of ripe grapes.

FAUSTUS. This is but a small matter.—Go, Mephistophilis; away!

[*Exit* MEPHISTOPHILIS.]

Madam, I will do more than this for your content.

---

[298] *Rid*: So 4to 1616.—2tos 1624, 1631, "ride."

[299] *That enchanted castle in the air*: This is not mentioned in the earlier play: but see
The History of Doctor Faustus, Chap xl,—"How Doctor Faustus through his charmes
made a great Castle in presence of the Duke of Anholt."

[300] *Delighted*: So 4to 1616.—2tos 1624, 1631, "delighteth."

[301] *It pleaseth*: So 4to 1616.—2tos 1624, 1631, "it *hath pleased*."

[*Re-Enter* MEPHISTOPHILIS *with grapes.*]

Here now, taste you these: they should be good, for they come[302]
from a far country, I can tell you.

DUKE. This makes me wonder more than all the rest, that at this time of
the year, when every tree is barren of his fruit, from whence you
had these ripe grapes.[303]

FAUSTUS. Please it your grace, the year is divided into two circles over
the whole world; so that, when it is winter with us, in the contrary
circle it is likewise summer with them, as in India, Saba, and such
countries that lie far east, where they have fruit twice a-year; from
whence, by means of a swift spirit that I have, I had these grapes
brought, as you see.

DUCHESS. And, trust me, they are the sweetest grapes that e'er I tasted.

[*The* CLOWNS *bounce*[304] *at the gate, within.*]

DUKE. What rude disturbers have we at the gate?
Go, pacify their fury, set it ope,
And then demand of them what they would have.

[*They knock again, and call out to talk with* FAUSTUS.]

SERVANT. Why, how now, masters! what a coil is there!
What is the reason you disturb the Duke?

DICK. [*Within*] We have no reason for it; therefore a fig for him!

SERVANT. Why, saucy varlets, dare you be so bold?

HORSE-COURSER. [*Within*] I hope, sir, we have wit enough to be more
bold than welcome.

SERVANT. It appears so: pray, be bold elsewhere, and trouble not the
Duke.

DUKE. What would they have?

SERVANT. They all cry out to speak with Doctor FAUSTUS.

CARTER. [*Within*] Ay, and we will speak with him.

DUKE. Will you, sir?—Commit the rascals.

DICK. [*Within*] Commit with us! he were as good commit with his
father as commit with us.

FAUSTUS. I do beseech your grace, let them come in;
They are good subject for[305] a merriment.

DUKE. Do as thou wilt, Faustus; I give thee leave.

---

[302] *Come*: So 4to 1616.—2tos 1624, 1631, "came."

[303] *These ripe grapes*: So 4to 1616.—2tos 1624, 1631, "these grapes."

[304] *The Clowns bounce, &c*: 2to 1616 "*The* Clowne *bounce*." 2tos 1624, 1631, "*The*
Clowne bounceth." (In the next stage-direction all the 4tos have "They *knock again*," &c.)

[305] *For*: So 4to 1616.—2tos 1624, 1631, "to."

FAUSTUS. I thank your grace.

[*Enter* ROBIN, DICK, CARTER, *and* HORSE-COURSER.]

Why, how now, my good friends!
Faith, you are too outrageous: but, come near;
I have procur'd your pardons:[306] welcome, all.
ROBIN. Nay, sir, we will be welcome for our money, and we will pay
for what we take.—What, ho! give's half a dozen of beer here, and
be hanged!
FAUSTUS. Nay, hark you; can you tell me[307] where you are?
CARTER. Ay, marry, can I; we are under heaven.
SERVANT. Ay; but, Sir Saucebox, know you in what place?
HORSE-COURSER. Ay, ay, the house is good enough to drink in.—
Zouns, fill us some beer, or we'll break all the barrels in the house,
and dash out all your brains with your bottles!
FAUSTUS. Be not so furious: come, you shall have beer.—
My lord, beseech you give me leave a while;
I'll gage my credit 'twill content your grace.
DUKE. With all my heart, kind doctor; please thyself;
Our servants and our court's at thy command.
FAUSTUS. I humbly thank your grace.—Then fetch some beer.
HORSE-COURSER. Ay, marry, there spake[308] a doctor, indeed!
And, faith, I'll drink a health to thy wooden leg for that word.
FAUSTUS. My wooden leg! what dost thou mean by that?
CARTER. Ha, ha, ha!—Dost hear him,[309] Dick? he has forgot his leg.
HORSE-COURSER. Ay, ay, he does not stand much upon that.
FAUSTUS. No, faith; not much upon a wooden leg.
CARTER. Good Lord, that flesh and blood should be so frail with your
worship! Do not you remember a horse-courser you sold a horse
to?
FAUSTUS. Yes, I remember I sold one a horse.
CARTER. And do you remember you bid he should not ride him[310] into
the water?
FAUSTUS. Yes, I do very well remember that.
CARTER. And do you remember nothing of your leg?
FAUSTUS. No, in good sooth.
CARTER. Then, I pray you,[311] remember your courtesy.

---

[306] *Pardons*: So 4tos 1616, 1631.—2to 1624 "pardon."
[307] *Me*: So 4to 1616.—Not in 4tos 1624, 1631.
[308] *Spake*: So 4tos 1616, 1631.—2to 1624 "spoke."
[309] *Dost hear him*: So 4to 1616.—2to 1624 "*dost* thou *heare* me." 2to 1631 "*dost*
thou *heare him*."
[310] *Him*: So 4tos 1624, 1631.—Not in 4to 1616.

FAUSTUS. I[312] thank you, sir.

CARTER. 'Tis not so much worth. I pray you, tell me one thing.

FAUSTUS. What's that?

CARTER. Be both your legs bed-fellows every night together?

FAUSTUS. Wouldst thou make a Colossus of me, that thou askest me such questions?

CARTER. No, truly, sir; I would make nothing of you; but I would fain know that.

[Enter HOSTESS *with drink.]*

FAUSTUS. Then, I assure thee certainly, they are.

CARTER. I thank you; I am fully satisfied.

FAUSTUS. But wherefore dost thou ask?

CARTER. For nothing, sir: but methinks you should have a wooden bed-fellow of one of 'em.

HORSE-COURSER. Why, do you hear, sir? did not I[313] pull off one of your legs when you were asleep?

FAUSTUS. But I have it again, now I am awake: look you here, sir.

ALL. O, horrible! had the doctor three legs?

CARTER. Do you remember, sir, how you cozened me, and eat up my load of——

*[*FAUSTUS, *in the middle of each speech, charms them dumb.]*

DICK. Do you remember how you made me wear an ape's——

HORSE-COURSER. You whoreson conjuring scab, do you remember how you cozened me with a ho——

ROBIN. Ha'[314] you forgotten me? you think to carry it away with your hey-pass and re-pass: do you remember the dog's fa——

[Exeunt CLOWNS.]

HOSTESS. Who pays for the ale? hear you, Master Doctor; now you have sent away my guess,[315] I pray who shall pay me for my a——
[Exit HOSTESS.]

DUCHESS. My lord,
We are much beholding[316] to this learned man.

---

[311] *You:* So 4tos 1624, 1631.—Not in 4to 1616 (but compare the Carter's next speech).

[312] *I:* So 4to 1616.—Not in 4tos 1624, 1631.

[313] *Not I:* So 4tos 1616, 1631.—2to 1624 "I not."

[314] *Ha':* So 4to 1616.—2tos 1624, 1631, "Haue."

[315] *Guess:* See note §, p. 127. i.e. note 201 So 4to 1616.—2tos 1624, 1631, "guests."

[316] *Beholding:* So 4tos 1616, 1624, (see note).—2to 1631 "beholden."

DUKE. So are we, madam; which we will recompense
    With all the love and kindness that we may:
    His artful sport[317] drives all sad thoughts away. [*Exeunt.*]

    [*Thunder and lightning. Enter* DEVILS *with covered dishes*;
    MEPHISTOPHILIS *leads them into* FAUSTUS'S *study; then enter*
    WAGNER.]

WAGNER. I think my master[318] means to die shortly; he has made his
    will, and given me his wealth, his house, his goods,[319] and store of
    golden plate, besides two thousand ducats ready-coined. I wonder
    what he means: if death were nigh, he would not frolic thus. He's
    now at supper with the scholars, where there's such belly-cheer as
    Wagner in his life ne'er[320] saw the like: and, see where they come!
    belike the feast is ended.[321] [*Exit.*]

    [*Enter* FAUSTUS, MEPHISTOPHILIS, *and two or three* SCHOLARS.]

FIRST SCHOLAR. Master Doctor Faustus, since our conference about
    fair ladies, which was the beautifulest in all the world, we have
    determined with ourselves that Helen of Greece was the
    admirablest lady that ever lived: therefore, Master Doctor, if you
    will do us so much favour as to let us see that peerless dame of

---

Note from (Doctor Faustus, from the quarto of 1604):

"Beholding: i.e. beholden."

[317] *Sport*: So 4to 1616.—2tos 1624, 1631, "sports."
[318] *I think my master, &c.*: The alterations which this speech has undergone will
hardly admit of its arrangement as verse: compare the earlier play, see note.

Note from (Doctor Faustus, from the quarto of 1604):

    [*Enter* WAGNER.]

WAGNER. I think my master means to die shortly,
        For he hath given to me all his goods:
        And yet, methinks, if that death were near,
        He would not banquet, and carouse, and swill
        Amongst the students, as even now he doth,
        Who are at supper with such belly-cheer
        As Wagner ne'er beheld in all his life.
        See, where they come! belike the feast is ended. [*Exit.*]

[319] Goods: So 4tos 1616, 1631.—2to 1624 "good."
[320] *Ne'er*: so 4to 1616.—2tos 1624, 1631, "neuer."
[321] *Ended*: so 4tos 1624, 1631, (and so 4to 1604).—2to 1616 "done."

Greece, whom all the world admires for majesty, we should think
ourselves much beholding unto you.

FAUSTUS. Gentlemen,
For that I know your friendship is unfeign'd,
It is not Faustus' custom to deny
The just request of those that wish him well:
You shall behold that peerless dame of Greece,
No otherwise for pomp or majesty
Than when Sir Paris cross'd the seas with her,
And brought the spoils to rich Dardania.
Be silent, then, for danger is in words.

[*Music sounds.* MEPHISTOPHILIS *brings in* HELEN; *she passeth over
the stage.*]

SECOND SCHOLAR. Was this fair Helen, whose admired worth
Made Greece with ten years' war[322] afflict poor Troy?
THIRD SCHOLAR. Too simple is my wit[323] to tell her worth,
Whom all the world admires for majesty.
FIRST SCHOLAR. Now we have seen the pride of Nature's work,
We'll take our leaves: and, for this blessed sight,
Happy and blest be Faustus evermore!
FAUSTUS. Gentlemen, farewell: the same wish I to you.

[*Exeunt* SCHOLARS.]

[*Enter an* OLD MAN.]

OLD MAN. O gentle Faustus, leave this damned art,
This magic, that will charm thy soul to hell,
And quite bereave thee of salvation!
Though thou hast now offended like a man,
Do not persever in it like a devil:
Yet, yet thou hast an amiable soul,
If sin by custom grow not into nature;
Then, Faustus, will repentance come too late;
Then thou art banish'd from the sight of heaven:
No mortal can express the pains of hell.
It may be, this my exhortation
Seems harsh and all unpleasant: let it not;
For, gentle son, I speak it not in wrath,
Or envy of thee,[324] but in tender love,

---

[322] *War*: Old eds. "warres."
[323] *Wit*: So 4tos 1616, 1624.—2to 1631 "will."

And pity of thy future misery;
And so have hope that this my kind rebuke,
Checking thy body, may amend thy soul.
FAUSTUS. Where art thou, Faustus? wretch, what hast thou done?
Hell claims his right, and with a roaring voice
Says, "Faustus, come; thine hour is almost come;"
And Faustus now will come to do thee right.

[MEPHISTOPHILIS *gives him a dagger.*]

OLD MAN. O, stay, good Faustus, stay thy desperate steps!
I see an angel hover o'er thy head,
And, with a vial full of precious grace,
Offers to pour the same into thy soul:
Then call for mercy, and avoid despair.
FAUSTUS. O friend, I feel
Thy words to comfort my distressed soul!
Leave me a while to ponder on my sins.
OLD MAN. Faustus, I leave thee; but with grief of heart,
Fearing the enemy of thy hapless soul. [*Exit.*]
FAUSTUS. Accursed Faustus, wretch, what hast thou done?
I do repent; and yet I do despair:
Hell strives with grace for conquest in my breast:
What shall I do to shun the snares of death?
MEPHISTOPHILIS. Thou traitor, Faustus, I arrest thy soul
For disobedience to my sovereign lord:
Revolt, or I'll in piece-meal tear thy flesh.
FAUSTUS. I do repent I e'er offended him.
Sweet Mephistophilis, entreat thy lord
To pardon my unjust presumption,
And with my blood again I will confirm
The former vow I made to Lucifer.
MEPHISTOPHILIS.[325] Do it, then, Faustus, with unfeigned heart,
Lest greater dangers do attend thy drift.
FAUSTUS. Torment, sweet friend, that base and aged man,
That durst dissuade me from thy Lucifer,
With greatest torments[326] that our hell affords.
MEPHISTOPHILIS. His faith is great; I cannot touch his soul;
But what I may afflict[327] his body with
I will attempt, which is but little worth.
FAUSTUS. One thing, good servant, let me crave of thee,

---

[324] *Or envy of thee*: So 4to 1616.—2tos 1624, 1631, "Or *of* enuie *to* thee."
[325] MEPHISTOPHILIS.: This and the next prefix are omitted in the old eds.
[326] *Torments*: So 4tos 1624, 1631 (and so 4to 1604).—2to 1616 "torment."
[327] *I may afflict*: So 4to 1616.—2to 1624 "I afflict."—2to 1631 "I *can* afflict."

To glut the longing of my heart's desire,—
That I may have unto my paramour
That heavenly Helen which I saw of late,
Whose sweet embraces may extinguish clean[328]
Those thoughts that do dissuade me from my vow,
And keep my oath[329] I made to Lucifer.

MEPHISTOPHILIS. This, or what else my Faustus shall desire,
Shall be perform'd in twinkling of an eye.

[*Re-enter* HELEN, *passing over the stage between two* CUPIDS.]

FAUSTUS. Was this the face that launch'd a thousand ships,
And burnt the topless towers of Ilium?—
Sweet Helen, make me immortal with a kiss.—[*Kisses her.*]
Her lips suck forth my soul: see, where it flies!—
Come, Helen, come, give me my soul again.
Here will I dwell, for heaven is in these lips,
And all is dross that is not Helena.
I will be Paris, and for love of thee,
Instead of Troy, shall Wittenberg be sack'd;
And I will combat with weak Menelaus,
And wear thy colours on my plumed crest;
Yea, I will wound Achilles in the heel,
And then return to Helen for a kiss.
O, thou art fairer than the evening[330] air
Clad in the beauty of a thousand stars;
Brighter art thou than flaming Jupiter
When he appear'd to hapless Semele;
More lovely than the monarch of the sky
In wanton Arethusa's azur'd[331] arms;
And none but thou shalt[332] be my paramour! [*Exeunt.*]

[*Thunder. Enter* LUCIFER, BELZEBUB, *and* MEPHISTOPHILIS.]

LUCIFER. Thus from infernal Dis do we ascend
To view the subjects of our monarchy,

---

[328] *Clean*: So 4to 1604.—The later 4tos "clear."

[329] *Oath*: So 4to 1604.—The later 4tos "vow."

[330] *Evening*: So 4to 1604.—The later 4tos "euenings."

[331] *Azur'd*: So 4to 1624 (a reading which I prefer only because it is also that of 4to 1604.)—2tos 1616, 1631, "azure."

[332] *Shalt*: See note.

Note from (Doctor Faustus, from the quarto of 1604):

"shalt: So all the 4tos; and so I believe Marlowe wrote, though the grammar requires "shall.""

Those souls which sin seals the black sons of hell;
'Mong which, as chief, Faustus, we come to thee,
Bringing with us lasting damnation
To wait upon thy soul: the time is come
Which makes it forfeit.
MEPHISTOPHILIS. And, this gloomy night,
Here, in this room, will wretched Faustus be.
BELZEBUB. And here we'll stay,
To mark him how he doth demean himself.
MEPHISTOPHILIS. How should he but in desperate lunacy?
Fond worldling, now his heart-blood dries with grief;
His conscience kills it; and his[333] labouring brain
Begets a world of idle fantasies
To over-reach the devil; but all in vain;
His store of pleasures must be sauc'd with pain.
He and his servant Wagner are at hand;
Both come from drawing Faustus' latest will.
See, where they come!

[*Enter* FAUSTUS *and* WAGNER.]

FAUSTUS. Say, Wagner,—thou hast perus'd my will,—
How dost thou like it?
WAGNER. Sir, So wondrous well,
As in all humble duty I do yield
My life and lasting service for your love.
FAUSTUS. Gramercy,[334] Wagner.

[*Enter* SCHOLARS.]

Welcome, Gentlemen.

[*Exit* WAGNER.]

FIRST SCHOLAR. Now, worthy Faustus, methinks your looks are
chang'd.
FAUSTUS. O, gentlemen!
SECOND SCHOLAR. What ails Faustus?
FAUSTUS. Ah, my sweet chamber-fellow, had I lived with thee, then
had I lived still! but now must die eternally. Look, sirs, comes he
not? comes he not?
FIRST SCHOLAR. O my dear Faustus, what imports this fear?

---

[333] *His*: So 4tos 1616, 1631.—Not in 4to 1624.
[334] *Gramercy*: So 4tos 1624, 1631.—2to 1616 "Gramercies."

SECOND SCHOLAR. Is all our pleasure turn'd to melancholy?

THIRD SCHOLAR. He is not well with being over-solitary.

SECOND SCHOLAR. If it be so, we'll have physicians,
    And Faustus shall be cur'd.

THIRD SCHOLAR. 'Tis but a surfeit, sir;[335] fear nothing.

FAUSTUS. A surfeit of deadly[336] sin, that hath damned both body and soul.

SECOND SCHOLAR. Yet, Faustus, look up to heaven, and remember mercy is infinite.

FAUSTUS. But Faustus' offence can ne'er be pardoned: the serpent that tempted Eve may be saved, but not Faustus. O gentlemen, hear me[337] with patience, and tremble not at my speeches! Though my heart pant and quiver to remember that I have been a student here these thirty years, O, would I had never[338] seen Wittenberg, never read book! and what wonders I have done, all Germany can witness, yea, all the world; for which Faustus hath lost both Germany and the world, yea, heaven itself, heaven, the seat of God, the throne of the blessed, the kingdom of joy; and must remain in hell for ever, hell. O, hell, for ever! Sweet friends, what shall become of Faustus, being in hell for ever?

SECOND SCHOLAR. Yet, Faustus, call on God.

FAUSTUS. On God, whom Faustus hath abjured! on God, whom Faustus hath blasphemed! O my God, I would weep! but the devil draws in my tears. Gush forth blood, instead of tears! yea, life and soul! O, he stays my tongue! I would lift up my hands; but see, they hold 'em, they hold 'em!

ALL. Who, Faustus?

FAUSTUS. Why, Lucifer and Mephistophilis. O gentlemen, I gave them my soul for my cunning!

ALL. O, God forbid!

FAUSTUS. God forbade it, indeed; but Faustus hath done it: for the vain pleasure of four-and-twenty years hath Faustus lost eternal joy and felicity. I writ them a bill with mine own blood: the date is expired; this is the time, and he will fetch me.

FIRST SCHOLAR. Why did not Faustus tell us of this before, that divines might have prayed for thee?

FAUSTUS. Oft have I thought to have done so; but the devil threatened to tear me in pieces, if I named God, to fetch me body and soul, if I once gave ear to divinity: and now 'tis[339] too late. Gentlemen, away, lest you perish with me.

---

[335] *Sir*: So 4tos 1616, 1624.—Not in 4to 1631.

[336] *Of deadly*: So 4to 1616.—2tos 1624, 1631, "of A deadly."

[337] *Me*: So 4to 1624, 1631.—Not in 4to 1616.

[338] *Never*: So 4to 1616.—2tos 1624, 1631, "nere."

[339] *'Tis*: So 4to 1616.—2tos 1624, 1631, "IT is."

SECOND SCHOLAR. O, what may we do to save Faustus?

FAUSTUS. Talk not of me, but save yourselves, and depart.

THIRD SCHOLAR. God will strengthen me; I will stay with Faustus.

FIRST SCHOLAR. Tempt not God, sweet friend; but let us into the next room, and pray for him.

FAUSTUS. Ay, pray for me, pray for me; and what noise soever you hear, come not unto me, for nothing can rescue me.

SECOND SCHOLAR. Pray thou, and we will pray that God may have mercy upon thee.

FAUSTUS. Gentlemen, farewell: if I live till morning, I'll visit you; if not, Faustus is gone to hell.

ALL. Faustus, farewell.

[*Exeunt* SCHOLARS.]

MEPHISTOPHILIS. Ay, Faustus, now thou hast no hope of heaven;
    Therefore despair; think only upon hell,
    For that must be thy mansion, there to dwell.

FAUSTUS. O thou bewitching fiend, 'twas thy temptation
    Hath robb'd me of eternal happiness!

MEPHISTOPHILIS. I do confess it, Faustus, and rejoice:
    'Twas I that, when thou wert i'the way to heaven,
    Damm'd up thy passage; when thou took'st the book
    To view the Scriptures, then I turn'd the leaves,
    And led thine eye.[340]
    What, weep'st thou? 'tis too late; despair! Farewell:
    Fools that will laugh on earth must weep in hell. [*Exit.*][341]

[*Enter* GOOD ANGEL *and* EVIL ANGEL *at several doors.*]

GOOD ANGEL. O Faustus, if thou hadst given ear to me,
    Innumerable joys had follow'd thee!
    But thou didst love the world.

EVIL ANGEL. Gave ear to me,
    And now must taste hell-pains[342] perpetually.

GOOD ANGEL. O, what will all thy riches, pleasures, pomps,
    Avail thee now?

EVIL ANGEL. Nothing, but vex thee more,
    To want in hell, that had on earth such store.

GOOD ANGEL. O, thou hast lost celestial happiness,
    Pleasures unspeakable, bliss without end

---

[340] *And led thine eye*: A portion of this line has evidently dropt out.

[341] *Exit*: It seems doubtful whether Lucifer and Belzebub should also make their exeunt here, or whether they remain to witness the catastrophe.

[342] *Hell-Pains*: So 4tos 1624, 1631.—2to 1616 "hels *paines*."

Hadst thou affected sweet divinity,
Hell or the devil had had no power on thee:
Hadst thou kept on that way, Faustus, behold,

[*Music, while a throne descends.*]

In what resplendent glory thou hadst sit[343]
In yonder throne, like those bright-shining saints,
And triumph'd over hell! That hast thou lost;
And now, poor soul, must thy good angel leave thee:
The jaws of hell are open[344] to receive thee.

[*Exit. The throne ascends.*]

EVIL ANGEL. Now, Faustus, let thine eyes with horror stare

[*Hell is discovered.*]

Into that vast perpetual torture-house:
There are the Furies tossing damned souls
On burning forks; there bodies boil[345] in lead;
There are live quarters broiling on the coals,
That ne'er can die; this ever-burning chair
Is for o'er-tortur'd souls to rest them in;
These that are fed with sops of flaming fire,
Were gluttons, and lov'd only delicates,
And laugh'd to see the poor starve at their gates:
But yet all these are nothing; thou shalt see
Ten thousand tortures that more horrid be.
FAUSTUS. O, I have seen enough to torture me!
EVIL ANGEL. Nay, thou must feel them, taste the smart of all:
He that loves pleasure must for pleasure fall:
And so I leave thee, Faustus, till anon;
Then wilt thou tumble in confusion.

[*Exit. Hell disappears.—The clock strikes eleven.*]

FAUSTUS. O Faustus,
Now hast thou but one bare hour to live,
And then thou must be damn'd perpetually!
Stand still, you ever-moving spheres of heaven,

---

[343] *Sit*: So 4tos 1624, 1631.—2to 1616 "set."
[344] *Are open*: So 4to 1616.—2tos 1624, 1631, "is readie."
[345] *Boil*: So 4tos 1624, 1631.—2to 1616 "broyle."

That time may cease, and midnight never come;
Fair Nature's eye, rise, rise again, and make
Perpetual day; or let this hour be but
A year, a month, a week, a natural day,
That Faustus may repent and save his soul!
O lente, lente currite, noctis equi!
The stars move still, time runs, the clock will strike,
The devil will come, and Faustus must be damn'd.
O, I'll leap up to heaven!—Who pulls me down?—
See, where Christ's blood streams in the firmament![346]
One drop of blood will save me: O my Christ!—
Rend not my heart for naming of my Christ;
Yet will I call on him: O, spare me, Lucifer!—
Where is it now? 'tis gone:
And, see, a threatening arm, an[347] angry brow!
Mountains and hills, come, come, and fall on me,
And hide me from the heavy wrath of heaven!
No!
Then will I headlong run into the earth:
Gape, earth! O, no, it will not harbour me!
You stars that reign'd at my nativity,
Whose influence hath[348] allotted death and hell,
Now draw up Faustus, like a foggy mist,
Into the entrails of yon[349] labouring cloud[s],
That, when you[350] vomit forth into the air,
My limbs may issue from your smoky mouths;
But let my soul mount and ascend to heaven!

[*The clock strikes the half-hour.*]

O, half the hour is past! 'twill all be past anon.
O, if[351] my soul must suffer for my sin,

---

[346] *See, where Christ's blood streams in the firmament*: So 4tos 1624, 1631.—Not in 4to 1616.

[347] *An*: So 4to 1616.—2tos 1624, 1631, "and."

[348] *Hath*: So 4to 1616.—2tos 1624, 1631, "haue."

[349] *Yon*: So 4to 1616.—2tos 1624, 1631, "your."

[350] *You, &c.*: See note.

Note from (Doctor Faustus, from the quarto of 1604):

"That, when you, &c.: So all the old eds.; and it is certain that awkward changes of person are sometimes found in passages of our early poets: but qy.,—

"That, when *they* vomit forth into the air,
My limbs may issue from *their* smoky mouths," &c.?"

Impose some end to my incessant pain;
Let Faustus live in hell a thousand years,
A hundred thousand, and at last[352] be sav'd!
No end is limited to damned souls.
Why wert thou not a creature wanting soul?
Or why is this immortal that thou hast?
O, Pythagoras' metempsychosis, were that true,
This soul should fly from me, and I be chang'd
Into some brutish beast! all beasts are happy,
For, when they die,
Their souls are soon dissolv'd in elements;
But mine must live still to be plagu'd in hell.
Curs'd be the parents that engender'd me!
No, Faustus, curse thyself, curse Lucifer
That hath depriv'd thee of the joys of heaven.

[*The clock strikes twelve.*]

It strikes, it strikes! Now, body, turn to air,
Or Lucifer will bear thee quick to hell!
O soul, be chang'd into small water-drops,
And fall into the ocean, ne'er be found!

[*Thunder. Enter* DEVILS.]

O, mercy, heaven! look not so fierce on me!
Adders and serpents, let me breathe a while!
Ugly hell, gape not! come not, Lucifer!
I'll burn my books!—O Mephistophilis!

[*Exeunt* DEVILS *with* FAUSTUS.]

[*Enter* SCHOLARS.[353]]

---

[351] *O, if, &c.*: 2to 1604, in the corresponding passage, has "*Oh,* God, *if,*" &c. (see note.), and that reading seems necessary for the sense.

Note from (Doctor Faustus, from the quarto of 1604):

"Ah, half the hour is past! 'twill all be past anon
O God,
If thou wilt not have mercy on my soul,
Yet for Christ's sake, whose blood hath ransom'd me,
Impose some end to my incessant pain;" etc.

[352] *At last*: So 4to 1616.—2tos 1624, 1631, "*at* the *last.*"

[353] *Enter Scholars*: Here, of course, a change of scene is supposed. (This is not in the earlier play.)

FIRST SCHOLAR. Come, gentlemen, let us go visit Faustus,
    For such a dreadful night was never seen;
    Since first the world's creation did begin,
    Such fearful shrieks and cries were never heard:
    Pray heaven the doctor have escap'd the danger.
SECOND SCHOLAR.
    O, help us, heaven![354] see, here are Faustus' limbs,
    All torn asunder by the hand of death!
THIRD SCHOLAR.
    The devils whom Faustus serv'd have[355] torn him thus;
    For, twixt the hours of twelve and one, methought,
    I heard him shriek and call aloud for help;
    At which self[356] time the house seem'd all on fire
    With dreadful horror of these damned fiends.
SECOND SCHOLAR. Well, gentlemen, though Faustus' end be such
    As every Christian heart laments to think on,
    Yet, for he was a scholar once admir'd
    For wondrous knowledge in our German schools,
    We'll give his mangled limbs due burial;
    And all the students, cloth'd in mourning black,
    Shall wait upon his heavy funeral. [*Exeunt.*]

[*Enter* CHORUS.]

CHORUS. Cut is the branch that might have grown full straight,
    And burned is Apollo's laurel-bough,
    That sometime grew within this learned man.
    Faustus is gone: regard his hellish fall,
    Whose fiendful fortune may exhort the wise,
    Only to wonder at unlawful things,
    Whose deepness doth entice such forward wits
    To practise more than heavenly power permits. [*Exit.*]

        Terminat hora diem; terminat auctor opus.

---

[354] *Heaven*: So 4to 1616.—2tos 1624, 1631, "heauens."
[355] *Devils.... have*: So 4to 1616.—2tos 1624, 1631, "Diuell.... Hath."
[356] *Self*: So 4to 1616.—2tos 1624, 1631, "same."

Made in the USA
Las Vegas, NV
15 December 2022

62164049R00069